GREAT SPIRIT...
THE COMFORTER!

by Aubrey W. A. Weldon, J.D.

DEDICATION

This book is for my daughter, Virginia and my son, Eric. May you both live in peace on this earth and dwell within the Great Spirit forever.

Love,

Dad

<u>GREAT SPIRIT...THE COMFORTER</u>
By Aubrey W.A. Weldon,J.D.

Published by:

Aubre' Publishing
213 Knowles Avenue
Daly City, CA   94014

Copyright c   1993
First Printing 1993
Printed in the United States of America.

Library of Congress Catalog Card
Number: "93-90883"

ISBN 0-9638392-0-9

Edited by: Marie C. Paratore
Cover Design by: Michael J. Greeley

FOREWORD

My journey has been long, but fruitful in the results. I want to say to both of you that the path you must follow to happiness in life is narrow. The only road signs along the way will come from your heart. If you are to find joy and happiness in life, learn to follow your heart. I want to share with you a prayer I wrote on my return from India in 1988:

"The Great Spirit of love, peace and joy,the
source of all life, the undefinable something
within us and all around us, the will of all.
Bless us this day with thou holy breath.
Have mercy on us in our thoughts, our words
and our deeds. And when faced with illusions
and falsehoods, give us the strength,the
courage, and the wisdom to seek the truth,
so we may quickly return to love, peace and joy."

This prayer represents the essence of the lessons I have learned since passing my forty-second birthday. The lessons I am going to share with you in this book will help you on your journey in life.

I am thankful for all the people who have come into my life at different times, who have made a difference in a spiritual way. There are too many to list them all. I want to extend a sincere thank you to all of you.

CONTENTS

Chapter 1

In The Beginning.....

Love, peace, and joy to both of you. This will be my beginning with you on this wonderful journey of discovery. Life has been good to me. Let's see, where do we begin? I will start out by stating that all the current theories about the origins of the universe are wrong. You have probably figured that out already. You have heard a few stories about the end of the universe as well. The scope and size of the universe is noteworthy, but the concepts are not without controversy.

Based upon contemporary understanding, the size of the sun in our universe is more than 865,000 miles in diameter. Mercury is more than 3,000 miles in diameter. Venus is about 7,500 miles in diameter. Earth is only about 7,900 miles in diameter, while Mars is about 4,000 miles. The two largest planets in our solar system are Jupiter,more than 88,000 miles and Saturn, more than 74,000 miles. Uranus and Neptune are more than 30,000 miles while Pluto is only 1900 miles in diameter. So what? How does all this scientific measurement relate to you? All you know is that you are standing on the Earth, and you are trying to make sense out of it.

Can a scientist help you understand the impact of our solar system? Can a Preacher or Priest help you understand? How would you live if you really knew the truth about it all? You are so busy trying to make a living that just the thought of how the solar system works is uncertain, cryptic, and obscure.

A dear friend of mine said to me,"Only write about what you know about." I have accepted that advice. I can only tell you what I know as a result of may short visits to this earth. Is the earth our true home? No! The lessons given to me have made clear that the earth is only a temporary home. A short station stop, on a long, long journey.

As a young boy, when looking at the sky, I felt complete wonderment. Where did it come from? Sitting outside in the warm summer evenings and watching the stars was like a dream. While laying down in the cotton fields, as the sun blazed a 105 degrees, there were more thoughts. What is it all about? My other three brothers and four sisters would harass me because of my daydreaming. The questions still echoed in my mind. My nickname was "the professor."

How much did my father know about the world? He was always an angry man, a person with only few soft words for me. He was a big man who had a loud, mean voice. Sometimes, he would beat me for behavior I felt was acceptable. He never told me about the solar system. He didn't tell me much about anything. My father was not an educated man. He had a good heart and he meant well, but as a stern disciplinarian, he was cruel.

I never knew who he was, other than a disciplinarian. He worked hard and long hours in the construction business. With eight children to raise, there was little time for small talk and affection. I have learned to forgive him and to forgive myself for not understanding our relationship.

My mother was another remote figure in my life. She had a keen insight into human behavior. She knew nothing about the solar system. She believed in God and she spent a substantial amount of her time with church business. Morning prayers were strict rituals in our house and that included knowing the proper prayer verse at each meal. She was a little heavy on me with the rod.

<u>**In The Beginning**</u>

A firm believer in the "spare the rod spoil the child" philosophy.

When surrounded all the time with many brothers and sisters there is little time left for introspection. As a child and a truth seeker, it takes years to find out that state of mind sets the course of your life. Looking back, all the experiments that were attempted and resulted in getting into trouble were truth missions.

In one experiment, my mother's umbrella is used as a parachute. An eight year old using it to jump off a garage was too much air pressure. Then there was the taking of two or three nails a week from my father's prize nail box that caused it to become noticeably depleted over time. After my father's investigation, on a Saturday morning, there would be an arrest of a suspect, me.

What about throwing a chair at my younger brother in the house. I never thought the chair could possibly miss and go out the front room window. The whole incident was observed by my parents as they were driving into the driveway.

The most pleasurable moments at my father's first house was playing, alone, beside the house in the shade. I loved to build all types of wagons, trucks, and buses. You can see the need for many nails. The kind of games played by myself would be about people going to work in the cotton fields.

During cotton picking season, during the early morning hours, you could hear the workers outside. They would be shouting instructions about which bus to catch. Our neighbor across the street was a farm contractor. He had three or four trucks and buses for carrying work crews.

<u>In The Beginning</u>

You could make up to three dollars for picking a hundred pounds of cotton.

Playing with my little blocks of wood from morning to noon was my pastime. Crawling on my knees with all the blocks (buses) in a caravan and pushing them through the dirt. From the side of the house, to the front of the house, along the sidewalk or into my mother's flower beds, it was a day of fun in the dirt.

At the age of seven, my mother and father would take me with them to the cotton fields with my older brothers and sisters. When they showed me how to pick cotton, I didn't like it! The reality of the cotton field experience shattered my childhood play time and opened a new window of awareness. It sucked! They gave me a little "gunny sack" about three feet by three feet. It had a cloth shoulder harness. You placed your head through the harness and across your shoulders. Each cotton stalk had about fifty to seventy-five branches. Each branch had five to seven bowls of cotton. The stalks, leaves, and bowls were dry and dusty.

The object of the task was to take the cotton out of each bowl and place it in the sack;it was tedious, frustrating, and stupid. The older you got, the longer the sack, up to twelve feet. Saturday morning would come, the sun had not risen. Hustled out of bed by my father on to the cold floor, we looked for our clothes. Bodies reaching over bodies, stumbling in the dark,finding the light switch. We slept four to a room, two in each bed most of the time. It was four to one bed when we were smaller.

We would have these long arguments each morning about who "peed" in the bed, and who

<u>In The Beginning</u>

should suffer the wrath of my father for the horrible deed. The arguments would sometimes become physical if the pee spot appeared to fall between the sleeping spot of two or more.
When it was time to go, each of us was given an egg sandwich for breakfast. Bologna sandwiches were given to us for lunch. On good days, we received some cookies. As the car hummed along the highway toward the cotton fields, we all fell asleep on each other. When we arrived, my father got out first. When he opened the door, the rushing cold breeze entered, the smell of cotton and insecticide hung in the air.

We would all stumble out of the car with sleep still in our eyes, the cold air provided a wake up call. It was a rude awakening. Following our father, looking like baby ducks following papa duck, we walked into the cotton fields. Each cotton field was about a city block long and about two city blocks in width. He would line us up at the beginning of the field, each of us assigned to a row. We had to keep up with each other while my father and mother would be four to five feet behind us. We used to have races to see who could finish their row first. I never won.

Thousands of times my father yelled at me for daydreaming. Bird watching was more appealing to me. When lagging behind,my father would shout at me, "Aubrey, get your head back down in those stalks." The sun would reach the noon position and the temperature would be around one-hundred and two degrees. The dust, the insecticide, and the heat were taking their toll on my sensibilities.
There was never a good time in the cotton field. One day, I came upon a rattlesnake. Across the fields and out to the main road,I ran, fearing for my life. There was about seventy-five pounds of cotton

on my back. After that experience, the trips back into the fields were even more precarious and life threatening.

In my fourteenth year, a friend of my fathers offered me my first summer job. Of course, I accepted. This guy would have done anything to avoid the cotton fields. The job was for an "Iceman." Up at three a.m. every morning, work until noon, return home to sleep for a few hours, and then back to work at four p.m. The day ended around ten o'clock. The schedule was tough. It was six days a week. Responsibilities included opening the store in the morning and closing at night.

Each morning the little dock office had to be unlocked. The petty cash was taken from the hidden location, and placed in the cash register. Next, unlock the Ice house, turn on all the lights and then load the ice truck, an old green 1954 Chevrolet, with six three hundred pound blocks of ice. I would cover it with a piece of canvas. Soon, the morning rush hour ice sales would begin.

Also, a three hundred pound block of ice was chooped into various sizes inside the ice house. They were stacked in rows. Fifteen pounds, twenty-five pounds, and fifty pound blocks were lined up in three rows. They sold at different prices. My tools for the job consisted of an ice pick, ice tongs, and string.

All types of people would drive into the half circle driveway to order ice. Buses and trucks would drive up along the curb and shout their orders. Around five-thirty, the store was closed and the ice truck was taken down to "the road." It was about a mile away. The reference "the road" is how my parents referred to the location of the

<u>**In The Beginning**</u>

poor section of town. It was where the minorities had their business operations.

There were several liquor stores, a grocery store, night clubs, and pool halls. It was a real "tin pan alley" of life's rejects. The truck was parked on the corner in the middle of the buses and trucks. Large crowds would rove about, looking for the contractor who was paying the highest wages. Depending on the season, work was picking cotton, potatoes or grapes.

The owners and drivers of the buses would come to me and buy ice. It was loaded onto their buses. Cars also would stop for ice. Around six a.m., all the buses and trucks would start for the fields. It was difficult to forget the smell of old wine, vomit, and stale urine. It was the smell of a desperate and illiterate people. The harsh sting of tobacco smells, dirty clothes, and body odor hung in the air. After the buses and trucks left, I would cover the back of my truck, lock up and walk across the street to have breakfast.

Mom's Cafe was the name of my morning break place. I would play some music on the jukebox, sip my coffee, and watch the last of the workers dwindle out. My pockets were full of money from the morning sales. It felt good to set there and feel the sun slowly rising outside the window.

Upon returning to the ice house, around seven-thirty, the store was opened for business. Just before ten a.m., the truck was loaded with three or four three hundred pound blocks of ice. It was time to do my ice route. This was the home delivery part of my job. There were homes and apartments along my route. The route was finished around noon. The owner would relieve me at the store. All the money would be turned over to him. Then it was time to go home to eat and sleep. This was my summer job until my junior year in high school. By the way, there was never a license for me to drive while doing this job. To to drive without a license was illegal. The owner and my parents were aware of it, yet they permitted it. Maybe it was just a sign of the times.

Most of the money from the job was given to my mother. She would give me some spending money for food and clothes. There was little time to search for the truth while working. There was much to learn about sex, smoking, story telling, and how to run a business.

At the age of sixteen,the Bakersfield Gospel Singers wanted me to be their bus driver. On Sundays, they appeared at different churches in the area. One time, they had me drive them to Los Angeles. What a rush of excitement. They also let me drive them to Las Vegas.

The group had a radio show on KWAC Radio on Sunday mornings. The man who was in charge of the group, Mr. Nicholas, really liked me. He felt that he could depend upon me. He asked me to come down to visit the radio station and watch the radio program. The radio station played country and western music during the week, and gospel music on Sunday mornings. It wasn't long before they had me playing the records,making tapes for commercials, and checking the radio transmitter.

They permitted me the use of the bus to take my boy scout troops on camping trips. As scoutmaster for two different troops of children from single-parent homes, there was a need for a lot of attention.

<u>**In The Beginning**</u>

Once we went on a camping trip to a camp located in the Tehachapi mountains. The bus lost its brakes on the way up a steep hill. There were sixteen boys on the bus. The bus started to roll back down the hill. There was a mountain on the right side, and a steep drop on the left side of the narrow road. It was a real struggle with the steering wheel to keep the bus from going over the side. By banking it next to the mountain, it stopped. The boys were taken off the bus and moved up the hill away from the bus. We placed large rocks behind the wheels to keep it from rolling any farther down the hill. We hiked into camp and called for help.

One Summer, a rumor was circulating throughout our neighborhood that the radio station was going to change to a rhythm and blues format. They were going to play gospel and jazz as well. The new program director, Mike Allen, who was a six foot eight inch AfroAmerican, came from Los Angeles.

One Sunday morning,he came by the radio station. He asked me if I wanted to be a disc jockey. I didn't know what he was talking about but listened with interest. He said that he wanted me to announce records, play jazz from midnight to six a.m. On Sundays, I played rhythm and blues from 2 p.m. to six p.m. He changed my name to "Art Weldon," and it was show time! After a few months, the people called me a "local talent" in town. Music and love became one for me. The response from my listeners was overwhelming. A Third Class Federal Communication Commission License was required to work on the radio. I passed the test.

It was such a joy to put together different

<u>**In The Beginning**</u>

musical sounds and experience the spiritual high. My air theme was the "original jock who liked to rock." The female attention was dynamite and my love for life skyrocketed beyond belief. The spiritual ramification of the experience was not understood until much later in life. It turned out to be a path that would open my mind, body, and soul to the dynamics of the human potential in the Universe.

While working in radio, I became a newspaper reporter. As a string reporter for a small newspaper called "The Outlook,"news reporting became my job. The publisher, Mrs. Green, gave me the opportunity to write editorials and report on local social events. Years later, the articles printed were kept in the Bakersfield City Library. Most of the stories and pictures were about the poor economic conditions of minorities and how it was in conflict with the American Dream. They tried to educate the people about the horrible conditions associated with poverty.

The editorials stress the value of Americanism and how African-Americans must struggle to get their piece of the dream. The writer was a messenger and a teacher. It was wonderful to hear the peoples response, though most of the poor people could not read, the pictures spoke for themselves. The lesson learned then was the power of the press.

I was eighteen years old when my first serious heart break happened from a relationship with a woman. She was a young Mexican-American girl who worked at a local restaurant. She had a little girl and they were from Texas. When she met my parents, their reaction to her was friendly. My parents never spoke against the relationship. It was time for me to learn the most crushing lesson in life, the male-female ritual dance of disaster. When that relationship ended, the military entered my life. There is more to say about this drama later.

Work did not end while in high school. Music was my major, band and choir became my love. Without strong academic talents, college was not supposed to be in my future. They had me on a low achiever academic track that lead to nowhere. According to the current conventional wisdom about educational opportunities for minorities, it was the right track. The train was sitting on blocks.

A happy person by nature, my love of music would become the saving grace of my life. My spirit was a friendly one and would easily mix with all races. The high point of high school was getting elected Vice-President of a student body of more than four thousand students.The first minority to achieve such an honor. They also gave me a two hundred dollar prize for being the most outstanding student upon graduation.

In academic subjects, only a few minorities would excel. Most were part of the deadly game of moving minorities through school as a social mission. Entering Junior College was a good idea. All my friends went there, and being around my friends was important to me. Junior College was the safety net or a spring board for poorly prepared students. In college, my major was music the first year. A job was an absolute necessity to pay for college. One day, before graduating from high school, a school bus approached the campus and it had an African-American as a driver. It was a shock at first. Then it became amazement leading to delight. That was the job for me.

<u>In The Beginning</u>

Once again, my love affair with buses started. My new job was driving a school bus in the mornings and evenings. During the day there were college classes. It was a great job! My first route was in the country picking up white students. It was quite a shock for them. It was my first social experiment;the first African-American driver sent to that part of town. It made me a popular driver with all the students.

My major in college was changed by my counselor because music was leading to nowhere. After taking a battery of tests, my counselor decided that a job as a police officer would be better for me. She said that my test showed honesty and integrity. My new major was called Criminal Justice. She was right. After the Marine Corp boot camp in the fall of 1964, I was tough, motivated, highly dedicated, and I had honor.

The day your mother came into my life, my work schedule had me driving a school bus on a special field trip to Bakersfield College. It is difficult to write about this part of my story. She was a woman perplexed about the world, yet very high spirited and aggressive. Just sitting there, perched on top of the wall next to the steps leading to the auditorium.

Remembering what was first said to her is difficult, but it was a sincere and honest comment. As an open minded person when dealing with the public, because of my public life in broadcasting, it was easy for me to accept people on face value. You could only hope the response to you would not be negative.

Our spirits were similar, though our race was different. As a public figure, the race issue was never a problem in my mind. My heart was open to all people, even a perfect stranger. The meeting was energetic with mild debate. What was not spoken became the bases for the beginning of a relationship. The next day, there she was again. She was sitting in the patio area of the student lounge. She told me that she had a boyfriend of sorts. He was a Jewish guy; the relationship was only lukewarm.

After that second meeting, she started to listen to my radio show. She would come to the station and watch me. We would take long rides in my little 59 MGA convertible. One day while with her in the school parking lot, her mother came to pick her up. She introduced me to her. Her mother's fixed gaze at me was cold and contemptuous. There was too much love in me to even care. There was just a strong sense of wonderment.

Shortly after that scene, our relationship became hot and heavy. We even did the "wild thing." We became inseparable. After graduating with a degree in Police Science, the plan was to move to Los Angeles and live with my Aunt. The goal was to find employment with the Los Angeles Police Department.   Our love affair was now by long distance telephone conversations. We talked most nights. She had taken a job with Pacific Telephone as a long distance operator.

One night, I proposed to her over the telephone with verse from a popular song. I said,"If I were a carpenter and you were a lady, would you marry me anyway, would you have my baby!" She said: "Yes!" Shortly after that conversation, she decided to move to Los Angeles. I was glad she did because Los Angeles had too many young women on the prowl and my over active libido was not mature.

<u>In The Beginning</u>

Honesty was important to me concerning sexual freedom. We knew nothing about sex in our family. It wasn't condemned,there was just a pregnant silence. Sexual inhibitions were lacking, so sexual development was primitive and experimental. Was there sexual abuse in our family? Yes! Sexual abuse in the sense there were no rules. When the energy was present, it would work itself out in a somewhat bizarre fashion. Let's say that we were either stupid or free.

Anyway, your mother moved to Los Angeles. She rented an apartment close to where she worked. One evening, while visiting her, she had her father on the phone. We had not met,nor would I ever meet him. It was the first time I was attacked for being an African-American. A few times, while in high school, race popped up in a rather unexpected way. He talked for a short time. He called me a nigger and threaten to kill me. He was from Mississippi and didn't like niggers.
I was shocked to hear what he said, but it didn't matter to me. I did not abuse him with name calling in return. I had a sense of pure wonderment. I just didn't get it. There was no room in my heart for racial hatred. My heart did not know what to feel.

The place where we grew up was segregated by race. We were surrounded by Mexican Americans and other African-Americans. My experience in my mother's church was different. The name of it was the Church of God, it was an integrated church. The ministers or preachers were of different races. On Sunday mornings, we would watch the members greet each other. The women would kiss each other on the mouth. The men would hug each other. They were different races. We never knew from one Sunday to the next whether the preacher was going to be African- American or white.

We never really thought about color. We didn't realize how unique it was to be in a racist society and not be **soiled** by it. I didn't care much for church, too boring for me. They wanted us to feel horrible because we refuse to repent and be saved. There wasn't much logic to their arguments. They tried to scare the hell out of us.

The taking of the police examination, and marriage happened in about the same time frame. Though the written examination and oral portions were passed, I had trouble with the physical. My teeth were rotten. Oral surgery was necessary.

The surgery would take one year to complete. I continued to drive buses. Even television had become a part of my life. Yes, a television news reporter. After extensive discussions with your mother during that year, we decided that it would be a good idea for me to continue college while all the dental work was completed. My major was changed to Political Science-Prelegal at California State University ,Los Angeles.

My new jobs were driving charter buses and working as a broadcast engineer on the weekends. Engineer? Yes! I graduated from Don Martin's School of Radio and Television after completing a ten week course during the Summer. I passed the test for a First-Class FCC License in broadcasting. I learned a lot about electricity and radio announcing. The new skills brought a better paying job.

I had a lot of enthusiasm about my college

classes, especially my American Constitutional Law class. With ease, I grasped the arguments in the cases, brief the cases, and argued them in class. The classes in Logic, Political Science, and Philosophy were stimulating. Each class required a whole new vocabulary. One of my better books was, "The Federalist Papers." The writings of Aristotle, Plato, and Socrates were impressive as well. We decided that an application for law school was a good idea. After receiving my Bachelor of Arts degree in Political Science, my next school was the University of California at Los Angeles at night. Some English courses were taken to improve my writing and grammar skills.

There were more classes in the basics because of my poor academic training before college. Still only functionally literate, I had to take adult classes at night in upper division courses: Algebra, Spanish, Physics, and English. The academic catch up years were in progress. It's never too late.

The first application to law school was sent to only one school and was rejected. My scores on the Law School Aptitude Test (LSAT) were just above average, but it wasn't good enough. The test was taken again to raise my score. The following year, applications were sent to fourteen different schools. The non-refundable application fee was from a hundred dollars to one hundred and twenty-five dollars. The money game was now in progress.

Acceptence was won at the University of California, Hastings in San Francisco. If it was not for the Federal Legal Education Opportunity Program for disadvantaged students, they would have denied me a legal education.

In the late sixties and early seventies our nation

developed a conscience on the issue of minority disenfranchisement. This was after the beginning of the Civil Rights Movement, the assassination of a U.S. President, the U.S. Attorney General, and Dr. Martin Luther King. My family was oblivious to the social and political ramifications of what was happening in the country. We knew there were problems, but we were too busy working to get caught up in the movement. We did not care for politics nor were we involved in the social upheaval happening all around us. We were isolated from the real spiritual impact of the changes.

The main reason we were wearing rose colored glasses is because of the choices we were making and the roots of my family life. My father would have beaten us back into the previous century if he found us demonstrating or confronting police. The other reason was the joining of the Marine Corp Reserves in 1964. It was a six year obligation, training once a month and two weeks during the summer. The reason for being a Marine Reservist and not a regular Marine was because of a white college friend of mine. He heard about my plans to drop out of college. At that time we had the draft. It meant that after the loss of a student deferment status,you would have been shipped off to South Vietnam, the current war zone.

This good friend told me about the Bakersfield Marine Reservist, and the prospects of continuing college after six months of training. All my high school friends who went directly to Vietnam died in action. This white friend saved my life.

I was quickly indoctrinated into military life. My love for America was strong. Nothing could be done to impair my obligation to serve. There are

<u>In The Beginning</u>

no regrets about that commitment to this day. It made me conservative and less rebellious, but it did not stop my search for truth, my desire for justice for all people.

In my first year in law school, it felt like a roof fell on my life. My spirit, soul, and body suffered a complete lobotomy. It was difficult to tell what hit me, but getting tarred and feather may have been preferable. Solitary confinement in prison was probably mild compared to the rituals and depravation imposed on a first year law student. It destroyed me. The entire three year period was grueling and intense. We had to study during the day, at night and on weekends. Appalling, cruel and unusual punishment for the sake of democracy.

At the beginning of the second year, your mother presented me with a baby girl. Near the end of my third year, another baby was on the way, a tragedy of immense proportion. I had no real sense about what was happening. Your mother was on the pill at the beginning of law school, but somewhere along the way, all that changed. Her unilateral decision eventually resulted in disaster. Even now, the motivation for having children under the conditions we were living is still not clear to me.

She was working; there were student loans and special grants for me. It just didn't make sense. My bell was rung and it has vibrated with irony every sense. Before law school, a contract for my next job with the Marine Corp had been signed. The goal was to be commissioned as a Second-Lieutenant and to serve in the Marine's as a Judge-Advocate. That obligation was set it stone. Therefore, after graduation, we had to go on active duty. The California Bar Examination was given in

In The Beginning

July of that year. About a month before we were to leave for Quantico, Virginia for combat training, we received the results. They were negative! In hindsight, a snowball in hell had a better chance of survival than my chance to survive that test.

My preparation for the examination was short sighted and inept. Fearing my writing skills, I enrolled in a writing course to prepare for the examination. It stressed memory gimmicks. The course was a real loser. My roots had taught me how to make lemonade out of lemons. They made me determined to make the best out of a horrible situation. My sense of direction and balance was destroyed.

Marine Corp life was a tragedy as well. I was so disoriented and lost. The combat training, all the new faces and bizarre ideas were suffocating. Keeping some sense of self was difficult throughout the ordeal. Once out of training status, conditions improved a bit, but the stench of failure stayed in my heart. The Marine Corp permitted lawyers who had not passed their State bars to practice law as a Trial Counsel. This position was equivalent to a District Attorney in civilian life. You also could act as Assistant Defense Counsel with a member of a State Bar. I prosecuted more than three hundered cases in three years.

Most of the cases were for minor infractions of military law, and some were for serious criminal acts. Also, a major KKK investigation occurred where my role was as an Assistant Defense Counsel. Several minorities where charged with felony assault and battery during a near racial riot over klan activity at Camp Pendelton, California. Marine Corp life was demanding mentally and physically. A few attempts were made to pass the

<u>In The Beginning</u>

California Bar Examinnation while on active duty, but they were not successful. It caused a deeper sinking into a state of complete depression, living the life of a zombie.

In the Marine Corp tradition of fighting hard and two fisted drinking, there was excellence. Going through the routines everyday, working hard, drinking hard, being a good Marine. Another tragedy was in progress. Something was horribly wrong, the light inside of me went out!

After leaving the military, the relationship with your mother was trapped some place between the earth and the planet Saturn. My soul was destroyed,descending on a suicidal course. The jobs in civilian life were high energy users with low satisfaction levels. Not being myself, it left me vulnerable to exploitation. The suffering would not stop.

I blamed myself for what had happened. My early childhood and my later delusions about reality were all wrong. Unfortunately, those were the times when both of you were children. You had to be around a father who was a complete enigma, a mere shell of a man. Obviously, there had to be life after this classic Shakespearian tragedy.
All one had to do was find it. My relationship with your mother was combative. My job as the general manager of a large bus company, had my soul lost further in the quagmire of business management and escapism.

The thought of giving up on the California Bar was foreign, though never prepared to take it, there were attempts. Like a drunk trying to drive a car down San Francisco's famous crooked street, I refuse to give up.

<u>In The Beginning</u>

As the marriage further declined, your mother started to look for a way out. Her involvement with the Christian Scientist Church was being set in concrete. My life style felt like a person living in hell. My soul wanted out of life.

Fed up with the bus company, I quit! The dream had stopped. My life was unfocused. Time had stopped. Leaving home for about four days, wondering across the United States on Greyhound buses, I ended up in Henderson, Texas, the birthplace of my grandfather.

Reality came back into focus for me while in Henderson. My soul was about to begin a serious search for its roots and it didn't even know it. After riding buses all night and day, I ended up in this place, walking through graveyards, looking for the grave of my great-grandfather. All the stories my grand father told me about his childhood were all around me, the horses he used to help raise and his fathers work with horses. Here was the beginning of a new path, a new hope, and a new faith. No logic or reason about this course, only pure gut.

I made my way back to the Dallas, Texas Airport. A quick flight back to San Francisco, I was home. Finding a job was the first priority. Walking into my house, I looked at the faces of a startled family, a confused woman who knew it was the end.

We had taken a trip to Europe a year before this incident. We visited London, Brussels, France and Italy. My personal crash was the following year. On that trip, the real animosity and dissension started. She detested me and took every opportunity to berate me. We were very different people now. There was no turning back, it was the beginning of the end.

<u>**In The Beginning**</u>

The search for a job begin. The City College of San Francisco had an opening in their Business Department and Criminal Justice Department for a teacher. Teaching classes in Commercial Law and Criminal Procedure, my life started again.   A Criminal and Civil Evidence class was added later. My road to recovery had begun. Passing the California Bar became my goal. An additional job was needed to keep up with the bills.

I found another job would be in the private security industry. My police background was helpful. It would not interfere with my study plans and my teaching position. The position was as a security officer. It didn't last long, about six months. As soon as the management found out about my teaching job, they wanted to hire me to develop their training programs and to manage some of their security accounts. The position was accepted.

Making more money helped the home life calm down. There was still serious trouble in the relationship. Driving buses on weekends was necessary to increase my income. Even with three jobs, the goal was still to study for the California Bar Examination.

My search for my roots was still intense and compelling. The sign and travel deal offered by American Express was attractive. Pay as you go vacations became the vehicle for my roots search. Africa was first, the west coast of Africa, the roots of almost all African-Americans. I went to Senegal, Freetown Serra Leone, Abijuan, and Ghana. Also, a place called Benin and the Village of Ganvie. The goal was to see all the major slave ports where African slavery to the United States begin.

Your mother went on vacation to London while

<u>In The Beginning</u>

I went to Africa with a tour group. The flight from New York to Senegal was over night. The plane was full of Africans coming from Canada, and some were going home during school break in the U.S. The morning we arrived in Senegal, the weather was already warm. This was a French speaking country, a former French Colony. We passed through Customs into the main part of the airport. The Africans approached me speaking French. I kept repeating to them that I was American, not French, and that I spoke English only. They would walk away from me, baffled or look at me with strange and distant eyes. I was excited!

While in Senegal, we visited the Island of Goree. This was the place where Africans were loaded onto ships and shipped to American. More than 400,0000 Africans were taken from the Senegal area. At one point during the tour, the guide pointed to a large hole in the wall and said that it was called, "The Portals of no return," by the Africans. Africans pass through the portals to the ships after they were sold into slavery. One of the other tourists took a picture of me standing in the Portal. As the camera flashed, I said aloud, "I have returned."

We visited two other slave ports, St. James Island and the Castle Elmina in Ghana. My emotions and thoughts were beyond words. A sense of irony, confusion, and frustration flooded my soul. A thousand questions rushed through my mind. Why did it happen? Who was responsible? Can it happen again? The Africans were so gentile and nice to me. They were docile and accommodating. An instant smile at the first glance, a desire to be helpful. Yes, it could happen again.

<u>**In The Beginning**</u>

The weather was beautiful. The sun was intense and penetrating. As we travelled from sight to sight, the Americans on the tour were constantly bickering with each other. At one point, two elderly retired school teachers almost got into a fight. It was instant hate. The weird thing about it was they were AfroAmericans. Here we were among the peaceful Africans witnessing one of the remnants of American- African slavery, African-Americans fighting African-Americans.

The impact of the entire trip on my life was immeasurable. It made me feel better about myself, a new sense of self worth. The information about my father's roots was impressive. He was Mandingo. We talked with other Mandingos in Senegal. Walking down the streets, I saw other Mandingos who looked just like my brothers and sisters. I was paralyzed. The spiritual shock was overpowering. That place was just a six hour flight from the shores of America, yet for Americanized Africans, it might as well have been on the moon.

The horrible tragedy of America's role in the African slave trade is beyond words, a diabolical perversion of human nature. An unforgivable sin that will continue to have untold suffering for generations to come,a legacy of hatred, violence, and deception.

Upon returning to the United States, I felt a new person inside of me, a new resolve. During Black History month, groups asked me to share my slides of the African trip with them. Colleges and my Rotary Club listened with interest. Also, the experience was shared with my brothers and sisters.

Something else was lacking in the inside of me.

In The Beginning

My routine was still to teach, work, and prepare for the California Bar examination. The mail finally arrived with my acceptance notice into the legal profession. Both of you can remember the screams, shouts, and the tears of joy on that day. An ugly and brutal chapter in my life was coming to a close.

I was admitted to the Bar in the Spring of 1984. My father had died the same time the previous year. Though he was present at my law school graduation, he would not be present for this watershed event. Celebrating my admission, I was off to Brazil. In Rio, I had a wonderful and joyous time. In the fall of 1985, I went back again for Carnival. Brazil was now a part of my blood,in my soul. Viva Rio! The home of spiritual and physical bliss. The people were beautiful, especially the women. They treated me like royalty. I felt free at last. Rio, convinced me that there was nothing wrong with a strong desire for affection, for approval, for respect and for love. The African in me wasn't a problem, America was the problem.

When arriving back in the United States and going through Customs, the white Customs Agents would focus on me. Their eyes darting about, showing their prejudice and paranoia about Africans. The cold and calculating stares could easily be interpreted as racial hatred.
Maybe they were not thinking that way, in that manner, but what they were thinking was irrelevant. The power of the symbols around me that caused me to create that phobia inside of me, was intolerable. The mental programs in my head that were caused by the symbols of hatred was always devastating.

In the Summer of 1985, your mother announced

that she was moving out.
She had travelled a couple of times to London and Boston, allegedly on a mission connected with her church. Once a letter arrived from London from some guy she had met on one of her trips. The pain I felt was unbearable, though probably unwarranted, but the implications were not discussed to a resolution.

Later that year, I vacationed in Tahiti. Bora Bora is a beautiful place. Living in a small cabin for about a week, my soul was at peace. It felt heavenly. The Tahitians have a saying about Bora Bora, "After God created the Earth, he made Bora Bora for himself." I loved the place. A year later, I visited one of the other islands, Moorea. My girl friend travelled with me. A portions of the trip was paid for by my airline mileage program.

My girl friend was a sensitive and caring woman. We met in the building where we both worked. We had a great time, snorkeling, boating, riding a motorcycle around the island; we were like two children. Someone had said that the best antidote to a heart broken by a woman is to find another woman. There is a ring of truth in that statement.

After my first major legal case in 1986, there was enough money to get a used car and to furnish my home law office. Your mother filed for divorce in 1987 to make the desertion formal. I was served with the divorce papers on November 10, the Marine Corps'birthday. An unexplainable tragedy had ended, the healing process had begun.

As both of you will remember, my role was father and mother for the next several years. What a learning experience. I learned a lot about myself during that time. Anything was possible if one had the desire to do it. The going was tough and it hurt, but my desire was to make lemonade out of lemons again.

Your broken hearts would take a long time to heal. My goal was to ensure that you had a home and food to eat. You would have someone to watch over you, a commitment to finish a bad dream.

My search for truth still weighed upon my heart. I read different books about spiritual growth. Then came the trip to India. On this vacation, I went from San Francisco to Los Angeles to catch a flight bound for India. We stopped in Hawaii, Taipei Taiwan, Singapore, and Thailand.

We arrived in New Delhi early in the morning, New Years Eve. The atmosphere in India was mysterious. A haze of smoke that hung over everything. It smelled like burning tires. It felt like an extremely old place. All that ever had happened to humanity had happened there in a previous Age, the impact was sobering.

The next day, my driver took me to the tomb of Mahatma Gandhi and the gem shops in the commercial district. Poverty was everywhere. Dirt, dirt and more dirt on almost everything. Though they lived in squalor, the people's eyes were bright and focused. As a tourist, my accommodations were first class.

I travelled to Agra, India by personal car the next day because the airport was fogged in. The scenes along the road were from right out of the Bible. Women walking with large jugs on their heads, turban headed merchants riding on top of their camels. The snake charmers walked around with their cobra, flute, and a mongoose. They would charge money for a chance to watch the cobra and mongoose fight.

My driver was an elderly man who drove with his horn. All the drivers drove with their horns. What an incredible scene. Cars, buses, and trucks moving between sheep, camels, and elephants. What a rush! You had to have a strong stomach for this method of travel. We were on the highway for about three hours, arriving in Agra around four in the evening.

The Agra-Sheraton is a modern hotel with views of the Taj Mahal in the distant. After dinner in the hotel, I decided to get acquainted with the area. On the streets were a few tourist;the locals were friendly and unassuming.
The next day, was a tour of the Taj Mahal. The greatest monument ever built as an expression of a man's love for a woman. Awesome and over powering,it stood shimmering in the sunlight. Love manifested before me.   The stone, cut to perfection, the imbedded color stones shaped like flowers, every inch of it was a masterpiece. The feelings of that moment went directly to your heart, it would last forever.

That evening back at the hotel, in the lobby, there was a little window on the wall with the word, "Astrologer" painted above it. One of the newsletters nearby said that astrologers were licensed by the Indian Government. That struck me as odd. Imagine, astrologers licensed by the American Government, what a jerk on the mind.

In the West, astrology was to be avoided as mere crack pottery, condemned by the churches. Here,in a country where the government issued licenses for astrologers, it represented an important part of their culture. What a unique experience.

Looking inside the small room, you could see a bed that occupied the entire room except a one foot crawl space. In the middle of the bed sat a plump, round faced man. He was wearing a white robe and a red scarf. He had three or four large books spread out in from of him. I asked him how much was it to have a chart prepared. He said," forty American dollars." I said, "Will you do my chart?" He said, "Yes." He asked me to remove my shoes and climb onto the bed. Then he ask me for my name, date and time of birth, and place of birth.

Sitting there for about twenty minutes, I watched him go from book to book making calculations. Finally, he finished. He looked at me and said,"Now, I am going to tell you the story of your life from birth to death." He told me about my father and mother and the issues that concerned me while growing up. He told me about my two children, and my divorce. He said that my death would occur near the age of eighty-five. As he talked about my death, he reached for his heart to show the possible cause of death. I was startled.

My understanding of astrology was mediocre. My exposure had been from reading several books about it. There were some experiences that were unique. After reading a book on how to guess people's sign, I learned it could be done with about a seventy per cent accuracy. My resource was Linda Goodman's book called,"Sun Signs." It showed how to look at the physical attributes of a person and determine their sun sign.

Looking at the little round faced, deep dimpled

man in front of me, I asked him if he was a Libra. He said, "Yes." My ability to guess Sun signs was discussed with him. He told me that the reason it was possible was because of my spiritual nature. He said that if my life was to be truly happy, I will have to follow the spiritual path. Wow! He gave me a lot to think about that night. He gave me a copy of the chart.

The next day, we headed for a place called Japur, the pink city. We arrived there after riding all day. We stopped along the way at one of India's largest game preserves. My driver checked me in the Taj Mahal hotel. Sightseeing would take place the next day.

After dinner, I took a long walk into the main part of the city. A lot of poverty, streets in poor repair, and traffic running amuck. The people stared at me with curiosity but said nothing. The smells in the street were atrocious but you got used to it. A full moon appeared later that evening, so another walk around the city at night was planned. It felt strange and intriguing to walk alone in a new place. I had no reason to fear for my life, but some apprehension was present because of the darkness and very few street lights. The hole you could fall into was the greatest threat.

The next day, we went to the world's oldest and largest astrological museum. There were large outdoor structures that would permit the measurements of the movement of the stars and the planets. The world's largest sun dial was there as well.

We visited the Japur History Museum. Inside was the largest display of ancient weapons and military armaments. The brutality of the times was clear;some of the weapons were more than six thousand years old. You sensed that hell must have existed right here on earth.

We went to a large castle on the top of a mountain and had to ride on elephants to reach the top. The place was built for the Mahareesh. Tall walls fortified it against attack. There were flower gardens and pools. One of the rooms, where love making took place, had glass on the ceilings. The glass was cut in a style that when the lights were off, the ceiling appeared to have stars.

We also stopped at a rug and jewelry factory; child labor was everywhere. The sight was depressing. Small children scrambling about with tools and brushes,it was awful.

The next day, we headed back for New Delhi by car. The road was a lot better. It would be about an eight hour journey. We stopped for lunch around noon and arrived at the hotel that evening. My mind was filled with India. The mysteriousness of its way of life was settling inside of me. The next day was the trip to Singapore.

Prior to leaving, I purchased a gold ring with my birth stone on it which served as a momento to remind me of the trip. A little expensive but I felt that I would see India only once during this life.

The flight to Singapore was uneventful. One of the most modern cities in the world, clean, green, and efficient in services. The hotel was sixty-five floors. My room was hi-tech all the way. The electrical system was built so you would never have to leave the bed to turn off the lights, T.V. or to close your curtains. The phone system allowed you to connect with the world at the push of a button.

<u>**In The Beginning**</u>

The tour of Singapore was on foot and by train. The view was impressive. The train system, made by Mitsubishi, put our local BART train to shame, a real eye opener. The people in the Bay Area are way behind on the transportation solutions. They have to fight for every inch of progress.

We left for Hong Kong the next morning for a brief stopover. We arrived in Hawaii that evening and transferred to a flight to San Francisco later that night. On the flight from Hong Kong, I gained a clearer picture of where my spiritual path was heading. My beliefs in the spiritual existence of man was getting stronger. The true journey within was about to begin.

My days continued with teaching school, driving buses, and managing security officers. Now the flame of truth was starting to burn with more intensity. The reading of more books was absolutely necessary. My studies focused on the various religious teachings, new age writers: Shirley McLaine, Jane Roberts, Edgar Cacye.

Reading the teachings of Gandhi, Buddha, Tagore, Allen Watts, and the Bible lead my research. The thirst for the truth was seeking satisfaction, the desire for knowledge was encompassing my soul.

In the fall of the following year, was another vacation. This time it was going to be Egypt and Jerusalem. My heart and my readings were sending me to the East once again. Arriving in Egypt after a flight from New York to Paris, my heart was pounding in my head. Though tired and sleepy, I did not want to rest. The experience of Egypt, the other part of Africa was waiting.

The first tour was to the Great Pyramids. We

went into the second Pyramid. This adventure is not recommended if you suffer from claustrophobia. We had to go down about twenty-five feet stooped over in a narrow passage way. When we came to the end of the passage, it opened into a large colorful chamber.

There were bright colors of images on the wall telling the story of ancient life. There were two other chambers, one was for the coffer of the body buried in the tomb. Standing in front of me was a different world, the first kingdom.The Africans, called Egyptians by the Greeks, were sun worshipers. They believed in the afterlife. It's the culture that brought us the one God concept. The next day we went by bus to the city of Luxor. From there, we rode a boat up the Nile to the Valley of the Kings.

The burial grounds for the early Pharaohs was called the Valley of the Kings. We entered the tomb of Tutankhamun, the boy Pharaoh. Again, we had to stoop down and crawl into the tomb; the walls were colorful and impressive. A short distance down the hill from his tomb was the tomb of Ramses One and Two;the same type of design and colors were in in their tomb as well. We also stopped by a monument dedicated to Queen Nefertiti; it was a vast temple with statues and carvings from another world.

In Luxor, we visited the great temple of Sakara, the holy temple where the evolution of the spirit of man had been taught by Sages. Lessons on the solar system were presented within the temple;the journey of the soul of man was one of the subjects. The statues were humongous in size, towering over everything. I was in ecstacy.

I toured the Cairo Museum twice. It contained

the history of the Old Kingdom, the Stone Age and the Iron Age. The early Africans on this planet were astonishing in their culture. The way of life was bigger than life as pictured in their art work. There were no more words to describe what was happening inside of me. The truth was humbling.

On the day before leaving Egypt, my Rotary meeting was made up at the Cairo Hilton. The meeting was in Arabic so a translator was assigned to my table. He was the Under-Secretary of Agriculture from the United States, a nice guy from New York. This meeting was quite impressive and will always be a memorable moment for me.

That night was the midnight flight for Jerusalem. Only one flight a day between the two countries and this was it. The airport was swarming with poor Arabs outside the doors of the baggage area. A baggage search and questions by Jewish security personnel took place before entering the boarding area. After you entered, the situation was peaceful.

We flew into the Ben Gurion Airport around two o'clock in the morning. A group of us hired a taxi to take us to our hotel. My reservations were at the International Hotel located at the summit of Mt. Olive overlooking the old city of Jerusalem. The hotel was ran by Arabs; they were polite and helpful to me. One could walk down the hill and enter Old Jerusalem through the gate near the monument to King David.

Old Jerusalem, divided into six sections, represented by various religions. The wailing wall area was full of people praying. Walking through the Muslim Dome of the Rock, there were Muslims praying. Walking on the path taken by Jesus while carrying the cross to Mt. Calvary was an emotional experience. Standing on the spot where they crucified Jesus on the cross, my heart was heavy. The tension, the mood, and the human spirit inside those walls was clear and convincing evidence that something happened there of monumental significance. This was indeed a holy place. Your brain would not know it, but your spirit and soul did.

We went by bus into the desert. The Bedouin people were living in the desert with their tents and camels, as they did more than two thousand years ago.

We stopped at the Dead Sea. Nothing lives in the water because of the high salt content;you could not sink while swimming either, it was a weird feeling. Thousands of people were taking mud baths then washing themselves in the Sea. We left the Dead Sea for the Masada, the village on the hill where many Jews committed suicide to avoid being taken by Roman Soliders.

We had to take a cable car to reach the top. The ramp built by the Romans for their invasion is still visible. The city had a synagogue, a bath house, and a water system that was revolutionary in its technology.

We left the Masada and headed for Jerico, the oldest city in the world. Parts of the famous wall attacked by Joshua in biblical times was still standing. Excavation was in progress. Jerico was a small city occupied by Arabs.

We returned to Jerusalem that evening. The next day, we went to Bethlehem to see the birth place of Jesus. Soldiers were evident. There were a few small children throwing rocks at the soldiers but it was still relativity calm. We stopped at the tomb of Sarah, there were Jewish worshippers present. They were crying and praying.

The place where Jesus lay in a manger is covered by a church. Upon entering the church, you can go downstairs where the place for the manger's location was marked.

Upon leaving Jerusalem, an instrusive search of me was made by security.It will be in my memory for a lifetime. The Jewish Security people were vicious and obnoxious toward me. They went through all of my luggage and four different security people interrogated me. They took me to a different section of the airport and stripped searched me. Humiliated and treated worse than a bad dog, I felt that their motives were racist and cruel. To this day, I don't understand why. It had to be the color of skin.

After boarding the plane, the experience would not leave my soul. The women sitting next to me was Jewish-American with dual citizenship. She tried to justify the behavior of those *#**s. The emotional impact of that day is still lingering in my soul; it hurt. As a lawyer, a security specialist, and a teacher, the behavior toward me appeared to be racist. It may not have been, but that was my feelings at the time.

Upon returning to the United States, this incident was shared with only a few people. It was the darkest spot on my trip. It did help me to snap back to the mental reality of the United States and its relationship with Israel. There is a lot going on there that most Americans are totally unaware of; It's not all kosher. Learning to forgive them was difficult. It will never be forgotten.

In The Beginning

After being back home for a while, the desire to go further within myself was strong. The focus was on meditation which turned out to be the real turning point, the true journey to the fountain of truth. In my job as a Security Specialist, there was the pleasure of working with a women who had remarkable spiritual powers.

She introduced me to books about meditation and she stressed the importance of it everyday. She was twenty years my senior, but her heart was that of a child. Her vision and her experiences had put her firmly on the path of spiritual growth.

When going within, I begin to tap into a reservoir of power that shook the foundations of my soul. There lay a diamond in the mist of a barren desert,it was my true father. It leaves you feeling like a person with a worth that can never be taken away, a power within that is not of this earth.

After this year, my soul will have travelled on every continent (except Antarctica) on the earth. It has found the truth. Now, both of you will be shown how to reach that same power inside of you, the Great spirit...the Comforter.

CHAPTER 2

REASON, LOGIC, AND OTHER CONFUSING THOUGHTS.

Jesus said, "There is no TRUTH in reason. Reason is only reason." This statement came from the book, "The Secret Teachings of Jesus: The Dead Sea Scrolls". The importance of understanding this sacred truth cannot be overlooked. The word "reason" comes from the word "ratio" which means to compare differences that are expressed in mathematical formula.

For example, if you have ten horses mixed in with thirty cows, the ratio is ten horses to thirty cows,that is, 1/3. Reason is used to compare many different issues, people, or circumstance, but it cannot express what is truth. The conventional Western thought is that reason and logic is used to discover the truth, NOT!

Reason and logic are limited to the forms in which the arguments are structured. It does not tell us what is true about the universe. It does not tells us what is true about ourselves. The popular definition of reason or logic is, "When one draws a conclusion or an inference based upon a set of facts." Facts are all the phenomnon we experience through our senses.

Can our five senses show us the truth about the purpose of life? Can they tell us where life comes from? Can they tell us where we came from?

The Hindu defined thought as the sum of our experiences tied together by our emotions according to our beliefs. What we believe controls

our thoughts as dictated by our emotions.
Each experience we have creates emotions and thought. The thoughts we create from the experience will be set by our beliefs. It sounds reasonable and it sounds logical, but is it true?

Under this concept, our experiences will be explained by what we believe in. It is well settled that beliefs come from early childhood and are directly related to our self image. To find out how a persons thinks, you have to find out what was the content of their physical, emotional, and mental stimuli during their early childhood.

The Hindu teachers viewed our experiences as activity. From activity comes thought according to our belief. What we desire or want is what creates the activity. What we desire depends upon our beliefs. Reasoning stands at the center of the circle of thought, activity, and belief. It is the road map that we set our life upon to find the truth. It is a road map that leads to nowhere!

This process of multiple thought forms is the activity of the brain. What you believe becomes the reality you create and it dictates your thoughts and the emotions connected with the various thoughts. You choose the activity that will cause more thoughts to reinforce your beliefs. You will find later in our discussion that the brain is subject to error. It is susceptible to illusionary and delusional activity. It can be affected by defects in the senses.

The multiple thoughts forms drive us in our activities until we fall asleep. Some of those thoughts and emotions continue after you fall asleep and become dreams, the only place one may travel beyond circles.

In Western society rewards are given for your

<u>Reason and Logic</u>

ability to reason. That is, to look for ratio within experiences and draw comparisons, going from one scenario to another. Depending on your beliefs or lack of any formalized belief, you express the ratio in such a manner that it supports the idea you are trying to communicate. It has nothing to do with the search for truth.

Words, the vehicles used for reasoning, set the stage for confusion or clarity. The more words you know, the more complex is your reasoning capability. The type of words you use show the level of your reasoning power and the success of communicating your ideas. Sometimes you will find that reasoning called scientific thought is much more impressive than words used with layman associations of gossip, trivial and trifling matters.

Scientific reasoning follows a specific form. The words used in scientific reasoning are longer in sound and more specific in definition. This type of thought is different than the words used for everyday problem solving. It is often stated that a grasp of mathematical equations lays a good base for clarity of thought. It develops sound linear thinking skills and will make ones conclusions sound convincing.

The predicament with having too many words and multiple thought forms is that they separate the people from the truth within themselves, leading to confusion and destruction to self. Because of the fallacy in reasoning, some of the most important truths about self are lost. Spiritual unemployment becomes the condition a person suffers through in life. The use and misuse of words become a death trap for the human spirit.

Once there was a man who had an apple

orchard. The people would drive by the orchard and comment on the large leaves on the trees. The limbs were covered with leaves. The people would say to each other, "What a beautiful orchard, look at the big healthy leaves. He will have a big crop of apples come harvest time."

Harvest time came but when the owner sent his workers into the field to pick the apples, the apples were small, discolored, and sour. He lost his entire crop. One day, one of the poorest boys in the neighborhood came to the orchard owner and offered to prepare his trees for the next harvest.

The owner could not afford to pay much because he had lost his crop. He gave the boy some tools and left for a couple of days to borrow some money to pay him. The poor boy spent the next couple of days stripping the trees of their leaves and cutting off some of the branches.

When the owner returned and saw what the boy had done, he grabbed him and beat him. The owner was furious, he refused to pay him and threw him off his land. The people would drive by the orchard and look in horror.

They said: " Poor fellow, he is now completely ruined. He will have to sell his orchard."
Well, harvest time came and the orchard owner had the biggest apples in the county. They were large, red, sweet and juicy. He sold his crop for a lot of money. He found the poor boy and gave him a bag of money.

The words and ratio used by people are like the leaves that covered the apples;words and ratio can cover a person's heart (spiritual consciousness), keeping the sun from bringing light into the heart.

Reason and Logic

Reason and logic can have that effect on your entire life.

Of course, there are all types of living conditions that can further cloud the path way to your heart, causing confusion and disappointment. More often than not, the job you work at could cause words and ratio to cover your heart.

The struggle to make enough money to live on, the fear of losing your job, fear of getting sick and not being able to work are all conditions that can destroy your spiritual consciousness. The petty office politics, the traffic you fight everyday to get to work, and the constant haranguing by the media will drive you into further darkness.

There is one truth that explains all of these conditions. Failure to recognize this truth creates the potential for the destruction of your being. The truth that cause these conditions is as follows:

There once was a wealthy man who had a large estate. It consisted of large commercial farms, shopping centers, many high rise buildings, and a few manufacturing plants. The man had three sons and a daughter. One day, he called his eldest son to his office and said, "Son, I am going on a long, long journey. I want you to take my estate and divide it equally with your brothers and sister."

The father left on his journey. The eldest son called his brothers and sister to his father's office. He was sitting at his father's large desk. He said to them,"I want you George (second eldest) to take over the management of our father's estate. Keep track of all the property we own." And then he said,"Frank (the other brother), I want you to be in charge of all the personnel who work for us, and to keep track of the business supplies and equipment." Then he added, "I am going to pay you both a large salary. You will also have health benefits, paid vacation, and a liberal retirement package."

He turned and glared at this young sister and said,"I want you out of here. Pack up all your things and get off the property." She was cast into poverty. After a long time, the father returned. When he saw what his eldest son had done, he made him go live in the desert for many years until he realized what he did was evil. The estates on the earth are still not equally divided, and our father is coming back. He is not going to like what he finds.

The truth is that you have to struggle everyday because of the conditions created by the undivided estate. Both of you must be committed to learning the path way to your heart and not be a part of a condition that will only destroy you. Be aware of the power of word and ratio and their power to destroy your spiritual consciousness.

Now I am going to teach you some of the lessons provided by the teachings of the Ancients of Africa that went beyond reason and ratio. They were lessons aimed at the soul. A lot of this information has been lost to generations. The few who are aware of the teachings keep them hidden. There was a firm belief during the early stages of mans'evolution that all the people could not be taught the truth. Only a chosen few were exposed to the wisdom of the Ages;however, I believe that the time has come for all nations to be comforted by the Great Spirit.

The Age of reason and logic is reaching its

natural and predictable death. The time has come for all souls that will take up the truth in its purest form, and evolve to the next dimension of spiritual life. Once both of you have learned the lessons about the brain's tendency to error and create illusions, you will begin to understand yourself. You will find the real purpose of your journey through this life.

The early Africans had a saying: "Mankind stands in nature (earth) under the heavens - and struggles to understand both - without ever understanding himself." I have always felt that my soul returned to this earth seeking the meaning of itself. After many lives, it was ready to face itself.

The seeking for self (being) started at around seven years old. During that time, in hindsight, I noticed a strong desire and need to know about all things. Another incident occurred around the age of twenty-one. That was when I learned how to guess astrological signs. The trip to India, the astrological experience, was another indicator of my seeking to understand the truth in the purpose of human existence.

My soul wanted to know the whys and wherefores of it all. The trip to the holy lands and ancient Africa pushed the impetus for spiritual knowledge beyond all imagination; there just had to be more. As mentioned earlier, the real journey started with learning how to meditate. Learning to listen to the little voice within without judgment. How was my soul being affected by nature and by the heavens? The ancient Africans taught that we were on this earth to learn the teachings of the three masters. If the soul was to gain answers about itself, it had to understand and act on those teachings.

<u>**Reason and Logic**</u>

When I heard about the three masters, I thought they were teachers in human form. I wondered about their backgrounds;where did they get their education? I thirst for the truth. My soul had heard and believed that "the truth shall set you free." The masters were not humans, they were concepts and ideas about the environment the soul must encounter on the earth; the information the soul needs to understand how its affected by all the things in its environment. Once the soul mastered these teachings, it would come face to face with itself;it would know its essence.

One of the lessons the soul has to master is the affects of mysticism and mystics. How can I explain to you the workings of mystics in our society? This is not going to be simple. The soul has an existence separate from the brain and the body, yet the other two are the temple for the soul to live in and use. The soul has had other lives in other bodies and it carries with it the sum total of all its previous experiences. It has also shared in the collective experiences of other souls. I am sorry, that was a mouth full.

Another way of explaining it: the souls within each body and outside of the body are sharing the same inner environmental conditions. A mystic is able to use words and emotions to fuse all souls into one, causing them to share in a simultaneous experience, causing similar feelings.

The mystic can cause all souls to experience the creative force within each soul at the same time. This is called the power of fusion. The soul is vulnerable to manipulation, and if the soul is unaware of it, it suffers untold scaring from brushes with reckless manipulators, mystics.

The technics used in our society today to

manipulate the soul is provocation, evocation, analogy and parable. The parable was the best known device used by early teachers during biblical times. One thing you must understand before I go any further is that there are three types of conditions or stimulus which speak directly to the soul without language. They are: sound, smell and colors.

The soul's reactions to these senses are not readily understandable, but there is a reaction. We only see the end results in the behavior of the person. We will better understand this condition after I discuss how the soul navigates through the universe.

How can your soul be provoked? One of the most pronounced methods is the use of sex in television commercials. This is similar to waving a red flag in front of a bull. We have found through past experience that the bull reacts to the color red, and it can be provoked to attack.

The basic sex drive inside the body can be provoked to respond, even if the stimulus is false. The "Pavlov" teachings are quite relevant here. Sexual desire is such a powerful force of energy to be reckoned with because of its propensity to affect us with little or no warning. We are subject to its control.

The body's impetus for life operates on its own earthly cycle. The soul is unwittingly pushed into the sexual morass. Therefore, by using sexual illusions in the selling of the product, interposing a red flag, the spark of desire for the sex can easily be confused by the brain which relates the product with the sex. It provokes the soul into action whether it wants to or not.

<u>**Reason and Logic**</u>

Sometimes words alone maybe used to provoke the soul,i.e., cause passion to overtake reasoning and burn up the brain. For example, when someone calls you a dirty name or they slap your face and call you a dirty name, the red flag goes up. We used to have a saying when I was young. When someone called you or your mother a dirty name, we would say: "Sticks and stones may break my bones but words will never hurt me." This was said to overcome our passions or avoid a fight. We were wrong, words could hurt and all the fights were demonstrative of that fact.

The soul may be manipulated by evocation. This is done by story telling. A story full of emotion and drama will stir the soul. This is called evoking the spirit within the person. Parables were the most efficient way of arousing emotions during biblical times. Some stories can evoke the same feeling in everyone listening to it, where their backgrounds are similar.

There was once a man who owned a farm. He plowed the hard and dry top soil each year. The crops were poor. The land was so bad he barely grew anything. After years of suffering and near starvation, he decided to sell his farm.

A coal miner offered to buy the property. He could see that land probably had diamonds underneath the top soil. The farmer sold his farm to the miner. The miner found diamonds on the land and became wealthy. In order to find the kingdom of heaven, you must go deeper within to find it. Some people can not see the kingdom and will give it away. Don't be like the farmer, look deep into yourself and find the diamond within.

You should be able to feel the loss the farmer

suffered or joy the miner found. The purpose of the parable is to evoke the feeling of what it takes to find the spirit of God within you and what wealth you will find. Both of you can remember the stories told to you as children. Remember the "Little Train That Could?"or "The Three Little Pigs?" These were all used to evoke feelings and to teach lessons about life. Unfortunately, the soul is unaware of the manipulation.

In modern times, we still use parables and analogy to evoke spirits. As you know, analogy is simply drawing comparisons and making conclusions by taking related or unrelated events and comparing them for similarities. The brain, subject to illusion and error, can be easily mislead by parables and stories. The mystic is well aware of this fact.

The second master is called the symbolist. The stories and parables are sometimes connected with a certain symbol. The soul will react to the symbol and remember the story. Symbols are used to designate things in the environment to help the soul identify them. They are used to represent the connection between things and being. That is, the soul and all its surroundings,i.e., heaven, earth, animals, nature, and other humans.

Each day of your life, the symbolist will be at work. Your soul will be bombarded with various symbols that have taken on a meaning in your brain. You must challenge all symbols presented to you. Check the validity of its meaning and whether or not it contributes to the healthy growth of your soul. There are some symbols that speak directly to the soul. I will go into more detail concerning those symbols and how they must be processed.

<u>Reason and Logic</u>

The last master is called the geometer. Concerned with the property of numbers and the becoming of forms, it measures the nature of the soul's existence on earth. All things in nature count. How nature counts and how it affects your soul will be discussed in great detail. The simplest way to understand this master is to appreciate the fact that all forms in the physical world are conceived in the brain, and are brought into existence by the use of number.

For example, you decide to build a cabinet for storage. You picture the cabinet in your mind as having three drawers with small knobs on each drawer. You also visualize a place where a mirror will be installed. The cabinet will have four small legs made in the shape of a lion foot and will be gold in color, with brown trim.

In order to create this cabinet into physical form you will need numbers to determine its proportions. This is where the impact of the pyramid inch becomes important. The number used will determine what form the cabinet will take. The early Africans taught that the soul's journey on this earth is also set by number. This truth will carry you a long way toward freeing your soul.

Once you have learned how to control the impact of mysticism, symbolism, and geometer on your soul, you will be on the path to salvation, saving your soul from its tendency toward suicide. Learning to free the soul is to learn the divine meaning of life - the journey of the soul. You will have to get rid of multiple thought forms to begin to expose your heart to the light of true knowledge. Like the leaves on the apple tree that were blocking the sun from the fruit, the multiple thought forms must be removed to expose your heart. You will be required to go beyond appearances, illusions and falsehood, the top soil of life. You will have to dig deep to find the diamonds. You must learn to know your own heart (heart intelligence).

At one point in African history (more than eight thousand (8,000) years ago) the scarab (a little bug that creates itself inside of dung) was a symbol of the journey of the soul. It symbolizes the human who realizes through himself the element of his becoming and his transformation. The ability to experience the "cause" that created the soul, understand the evolution of the soul, describes the process. They firmly believed that the "cause" that caused itself and caused all forms is undefinable and unknowable.

Another way of saying this great truth is that the energy that caused life on this earth can only be experienced and can not be a product of knowledge. The brain can not label nor understand the nature of the energy, the Great Spirit. The soul is able to experience the Great Spirit, and the soul over time will commit suicide if it does not experience its creator. It will have to keep coming back in a new life until it recognizes its true father.

According to Gandhi, the soul is like a drop of water in the ocean. If separated from the ocean, it will dry up. Yet, once its aware of its role in life itself, just a part of all the souls, it will be free. You will find in all societies that all the souls are at different stages of evolution. I will mention this now, but later I will go into more detail. The evolution of the soul is about the soul recognizing its own perfection. It's about the soul searching for it own perfection. Imperfection is the state all souls suffer through because of the lack of experiencing its cause which is perfect.

The best way to see the stations in life where souls hang out is to divide the society into three circles, as was done by the Ancients. In the outer circle of society lives the souls that are governed by passion, they are trapped within the five senses. These souls can be found working as common laborers, farmers, government officials;some of them may be craftsmen, minor priests, and low level business managers.

In the second circle are the souls trapped in reason and logic,the brain. Here we find technicians, scientists, artists, master craftsmens;some educators, and other professionals.

The first circle contains the souls living by heart intelligence. Here you find the sages, the temples of wisdom, those with fire in the heart -the fire of life. This circle is referred to as positive reality, the second circle is designated as relative reality, and the third circle is the reality of the sense, the emotional world.

The third circle is unmanageable and has no relationship to the first circle. Once you have determined which circle your soul lives in, you can conceptually see your location in the journey of your soul. The Sages taught that it was almost impossible for the soul to get out of the third circle. Those souls in the second circle have the possibility of reaching the first circle if they are able to find their heart.

Now, I am prepared to show you how the senses work, how they affect the reality you are creating.

<u>**Reason and Logic**</u>

How do you interface with the solar system through your body?

The face on your body is your mirror of the solar system. It permits you to navigate on the earth and reflect the solar system. This may all sound elementary but there are some subtleties that can't be overlooked;the deeper meaning of the senses and their purpose.

The eyes are used to see;however, they also accept light and create energy. Ever wonder why eye contact with another person can be devastating depending on the level of energy being projected. The ears are not just for hearing;the ears are responsible for the direction and balance of the body when moving through space. The nose is thought to be only for breathing and smelling things. It's easy to overlook the fact that the nose also creates forms in the mind. The mouth is not just for eating, breathing, and talking;it also provides for tasting and experiencing different flavors.

It's the face that permits you to assimilate with the universe. The eyes receiving light, the ears permitting you to move about, and the nose creating forms in the brain. Of course, the mouth permits the sampling of the earth itself. The ancient societies recognized the impact of the senses and how they related to the creation of the solar system within the body. They used an analogy of the face as being the mirror of the universe. The moon is the mirror of the sun. The hearts role to the body is as the sun is to the solar system. The moon is like the brain and like the moon reflects the sun, the brain reflects the heart.

The Africans taught that the universe consisted

of five elements. Sound being the first, followed by fire, water, air and earth. Sound, vibration, was the first element of our solar system.

Vibrations can be found in all things. I know that this lecture is moving rapidly but you will have plenty of time to explore on your own. Modern science is still struggling with these concepts, trying to find the unified theory about the creation of the solar system.

The Ancients gave up on what caused it all;they felt that it was undefinable and unknowable and left it alone. The Western Scientist have reduced the search down to the atom, quarks, and the unpredictability of them. The Big Bang theory is popular today. That is, somewhere out in space, there was a big bang (atomic explosion) and somehow the earth and the rest of the solar system fell into place with the planets moving in their own cycles. We now have the expanding universe and we don't know where its headed. Some have even argued that the universe is collasping.

The important thing to understand is that all nations on the earth have some kind of explanation about the creation of the solar system and how life on earth is affected by it. I will explore some of those systems of thought later in this journey. What the Africans taught inflamed my heart with the desire to learn more,the sages in the temples of wisdom, marking each Age into the future.

In order to understand the system, we start with sound. The soul must master the affects of sound. Words cause the greatest problem for the soul. The Ancients referred to the word as the divine word because of its spiritual impact. Words are vibrations, and vibrations communicate directly with the soul. Words have a spiritual origin; that's why they are divine. The Ancients used to say that,"To know a things real name is to know its power. To pronounce it exactly is to free its energy." All words contain energy that is independent of the word itself.

The use of words and mysticism have a direct relationship. Before going further into the mysticism of words, I want to mention that there are three conditions we find in the solar system: harmony, systems, and balance. The three conditions can be expressed as: music, arithmetic, and geometry.

These three conditions are reflected in the person through, spirit, mind,and individual experience. All three of the conditions affect the soul. We use words to express the impact of these conditions on a daily basis. Each one of the conditions are expressed in the teachings of the three masters. Mysticism deals with harmony and disharmony. Symbolism is about system identity, and geometer is about balance and unbalanced conditions.

The soul of a person is lifted and enlightened by the spirit. The mind operates the systems in the body. Each experience the person is exposed to will have an impact on the soul in proportion to the gravity of the experience.

What makes the word divine? Well, divine is associated with the spirit realm. It means that words spring from the invisible and unknowable "cause." They spring from sound, the first cause. Silence is the nature of the universe. All things spring from silence. The word is a product of vibration and sound. The Ancients, in the development of their language, created symbols that represent things which occur in nature. This helped them to explain the functions of a thing by invoking the spirit of it. They also developed symbols that would explain the heavens. Symbols they developed contained the spirit of the thing itself,its function, its character and its feeling.

The symbol was related to a function on the body;that is, if the thing acted like a part of the human body, the symbol for it was related to that function. For example, the letter "b" looks like a foot and leg. The purpose of the foot and leg is to support the body. All things that had that functions in nature started with the letter "b." If this logic is consistent, it means that the energy or spirit of a thing is captured in its name. It means that you might use a name thinking that it means one thing but its spirit is associated with something else.

This entire area of research is new to me but I find it awesome. I will share with you what I have learned, but further investigation on your part will be required. I'm going to proceed through the Alphabet as we know it in modern times. When I used the term Alphabet, I'm simply referring to symbols. The early Africans referred to them as hieroglyphics.

The first is the letter "a" It was the symbol of the action-principle that signified the greatest to the limits of possibilities,i.e., great yield. It was identified with the number one which was also identified with the sun.

The letter "b" was taken from the shape of the leg and foot. When used, it was about something that supports.It was the sign of duality when two "b's" were together. The number two is for this letter and it stood for the moon. The letter "c" symbolized animated life, creation itself, symbolized by the number three. The letter "d" was about something that had reached its limits, it could go no farther. It is symbolized by the number four. The letter "e" designated movement and active appearances. It is about energy and was given the number five.

The letter "f" was to represent breath, the vital quality, the heart symbol. It was given the number six. The letter "g" was about the internal, within, the inside. The active spirit within. It was given the number seven. The letter "h" showed a crossing; energized reactively that which causes phenomenon. It was given the number eight. The letter "i" is the me-principle. It was symbolized by the eye;it was that which opens and shuts, receiving light and refusing light. It was given the number nine.

The first nine letters were seen as active/passive in energy force, and had a positive charge. The next nine letters are reactive with a negative energy charge, a constant stimulative.

The letter "j" represented an action principle that was reactive and dual in force. It was given the number one but with a negative charge. The letter "k" symbolized the animated breath, the quickening principle. It was given the number two with a negative charge. The letter "l" symbolized transformation or becoming. The number three is its symbol and it has a negative charge. The letter "m" is that which gives birth, to produce, to give life. It was given the negative number four. The letter "n" symbolized the creation of environment and the creation of duality. The vibration that reveals the content of the container. It was given the negative five number.

The letter "o" was the symbol for the rhythm of becoming and beginning. It has the negative number six vibration. The letter "p" is to show the place where something parks. The sky where the stars park. The home and direction of the path internal. It was given the negative number seven. The letter "q" was also reactive negative and dealt with causing reactive phenomena. It was given the negative number eight. The letter "r" represented the solar nature;that which moves in circles, dilating and contracting-open and close. It was given the negative number nine.

The previous set of nine numbers are negative and reactive in force. The last set of eight symbols are have a dual quality. They contained both negative and positive forces that result in a creative force. Each symbol associated with the creative spirit or vibration was set as creative force.

The letter "s" is the symbol of spermatic fire, the fertilization of the species. The germ that sparked creation itself. It was given the number one with a positive/negative charge. The letter "t" is about terrestrial phenomenon, life on the earth. It's passive force with a positive/negative in its affects. It has the creative number two. The letter "u" is about the all, everything, everyone;it's creative with positive/negative number three.

The letter "v" symbolizes the active-principle of creation, it is given the positive/negative four vibration. The letter "w" is to symbolize amplitude, growth expression, and was given the positive/negative number five. The letter "x" is the symbol for static, rhythmic vital activity. It is the positive/negative number six. The letter "y" symbolizes the animation of passivity, movement, and it's internal. It was given the positive/negative number seven. The letter "z" was given the crossing designation. It causes creative phenomenon. It was given the positive/negative eight.

You are probably wondering if this elaborate scheme applies to all languages? If it's valid, then it should apply; however, I strongly believe that different cultures have experienced the earth and the heavens in different ways. The vibrations they

felt ties into their language and symbols. The key to this question is in the numbers. All life is vibration. The symbols and language used by each culture will express it meanings in the forms agreed upon.

Now, you can take any word and find the spirit within it. For example, the word "life" means it's something in transformation. It's animal or human because it breath and it moves. How about the word "love?" It's about transformation of beginning and ending in a creative way with movement. You also notice that both words start with the reactive negative force.

The early Africans always thought that life was about the journey of the soul in transformation. The soul is on a voyage. "All existence is a voyage on a course of which the soul, carried in it's corporal boat, is impregnated with consciousness as your eyes with the colors, your ears with the words of nature." What determines the journey the soul will take? The desire and aim of the soul is what moves the soul along its path. What should be the desire and aim of the soul? Here's the crux of the problem with most humans. They spend a life time with many different desires and end up suffering dismal misery.

It has nothing to do with wealth. One fact about the soul is when it's distorted, suffering is equal regardless of station in life. The Hindu and the African's believed that the desire and aim of the soul should be to journey beyond forms and matter. That is, the soul should prepare itself to leave the body and join the spirit with ease. The soul should thrive to become one with the spirit, the light of the universe. I will talk more about this journey at a later juncture.

The symbolist was the second master for the soul to overcome to be free. One of the most important symbols on this earth for mankind is the symbol of the Great Pyramid in ancient Africa, the Greeks called Egypt. The Ancients said: "Unfailing witness of the pyramid that cannot err." That meant that the person who understood the lessons symbolized by the pyramid will know the truth about the journey of the soul.

The pyramid is a symbol of the limits of the soul's journey on earth. If a soul can learn the lessons of the pyramid, it will be free. It will have access to other spiritual levels of existence without the hardship of forms and matter. The pyramid is a definition of life on earth. The "p" represents the place where the soul parks. The home of the soul. The "y" means that it's the place where the internal environment of the soul lives.

The "r" teaches us that the soul is part of the

solar nature and that it moves in circles. It is dilating and contracting. The "a" means that the soul, acts within the form and matter on earth; it has great possibilities beyond the limits of earth. The "m" means that all we give birth to or produce happens within the limits of the pyramid. The "i" shows how we view ourselves. Each day and night, and the "d" teaches us that the soul reaches a limit inside the pyramid. That's why the desire and aim of the soul is to go beyond the pyramid.

The pyramid is the magnet that brings heaven and earth together. Its name is the way to revelations. It represents the descent of the soul into matter, the descent into the body on earth. It also represents the ascent of the soul from the body. In every form on earth you will find the pyramid. The pyramid is a cosmic truth.

The last master, the geometer, teaches us that the the soul must conquer the implications of numbers and where they come from;how they represent the truth of the solar system. How are they imitated here on earth?

As both of you have learned, numbers are a part of all types of deception on earth. They can quantify ignorance, manipulate the many by the few. They can set souls against souls, to make souls seek suicide in the body. You must master the vibration of number and recognize that they only exist in heaven. The sky is the home of the forces that we can't see but only feel their affects. As observers of the sky, you can take three positions.

There is first the affects of the abstract causal forces and creative ideas attributed thereto. The second is living with the process of becoming within, and lastly, the ability to see yourself as the final product of creation. Face to face with it, and to study each of its elements.

The soul must learn how to have insight into all three states and not to confuse them. The abstraction of forces from above brings about gestation and gives it quantity. Your own gestation is a part of this world and you become the final product of it all. For example, the sun is the causal force that makes a plant grow on earth. There is the process of the growth patterns within the plant. The final result of this activity is the plant itself.

The sun is the source of human life on the earth. There is the process of growth inside the human body, and there is the end result - you.

The sky is where numbers live. They impose themselves on all life in great and small cycles all the time. The cycle of the number 12 is significant. The star constellations never change. They circle the earth every 12 months. They travel from east to west. The creative idea developed by the

Ancients called this system of movement, the zodiac - the celestial stream. The Ancients divided the zodiac into thirty-six (36) sectors. Stars belonging to each sector were called decanate because each sector was in the sky for ten (10) days.

Keep in mind that this drama in the sky existed independent of what theory the humans on earth were considering. The only truth here is the observations. The application of number,that is, 10, 12, etc.,etc., is a man made connection.
To say that the numbers live in the sky, is simply

to acknowledge that man's rational brain has defined his sky by using a number system he devised. The system, based on the number 10, is established by the Ancients the same way they developed the alphabet. He referred to his body, in this instance, the two hands for counting.

This is why the sky, as an abstract world, becomes the definition of its cycles and causes many different types of numbers. The sun was seen as the master and lifegiver in the twelve (12) sectors. The star sectors moved in one cycle, while the planets, as observed by the Ancients, moved in different cycles and at different speeds, giving birth to abstraction of numbers.

For example, there were two planets that travel close to the sun, Mercury and Venus. By the way, the term "planet" means to wonder about, that is, they move about the solar system. Venus is present when the sun sets and when it rises.
It is in front of the sun at its rising and it is near it at its setting. Mars, Jupiter and Saturn move in the celestial stream, sometimes in reverse direction.

The sun travels through all thirty-six (36) sectors in twelve (12) months, Jupiter in twelve (12) years, crossing three sectors a year. Saturn takes twenty-nine (29) years to travel through the thirty-six (36) sectors.

The Ancients saw the moon as responsible for gestation (life) on earth. That is, the birth cycle in the female is set by the moon. The moons cycle is about twenty-nine days, and because Saturn's cycle is about twenty-nine years, the Ancient felt that Saturn represented the master of time and the lunar periods.

They believed that the whole universe is alive,

<u>**Reason and Logic**</u>

and is the source of every -thing; life itself is one with it, despite appearances. With this strong belief, that the universe was the causal source for everything, the ideas about life on earth and its relationship to the universe became the starting point for explaining nature and life.

Just like the sun is different everyday, stellar conjunctions are changing all the time. Each new seed on earth will produce another seed-unlike itself. We have daily seasons, monthly seasons, and annual seasons. Due to the cycles of the sun, the year is divided into three seasons. Each season has four months. The seasons are winter, summer, and fall.

The sun travels north for six (6) months; then it travels south for six (6) months. One hour in a day equals 1/12 of a twelve hour day, and a twelve hour night. The universe is counting, when the using numbers assigned by the Ancients.

With number, the geometer sets down the rules to use for the interpretation of the solar system. The behavior and appearances of the system is acting independently of the geometers findings. The number is the definition for a cycle. The following numbers are given to the rotational cycle of each wanderer in the solar system:

Sun - 25 days and 8 hours
Mercury - 58 days and 16 hours
Venus - 243 days
Earth - 23 hours and 56 minutes
Mars - 24 hours and 37 minutes
Jupiter - 9 hours and 48 minutes
Saturn - 10 hours and 39 minutes
Uranus - 17 hours and 14 minutes
Neptune - 18 hours and 30 minutes
Pluto - 6 days and 9 hours

<u>**Reason and Logic**</u>

All the Planets are rotating around the Sun at various speeds:

Mercury - 86 days
Venus - 225 days
Earth - 365.26 days
Mars - 1.88 years
Jupiter - 11.9 years
Saturn - 29.5 years
Uranus - 84 years
Neptune - 165 years
Pluto - 248 years

The sky is a world of abstractions interpreted by numbers. A dance that is so perfect, a number can be used to predict each movement.

Earth dwellers will concede that the sun has an affect on human life. They also accept the fact that the moon has an affect on human life. There are many different interpretations about the quality or nature of the affect. A great number of humans reject any notion that the great dance in the sky is affecting the nature of the human dance. A leap of faith is required to define and interpret other possible affects of the solar system on human life. This is where the geometer gets covered by mysticism and dogma.

The Ancients believed that nature and the fate of animals are fixed by the stars. Whatever happens to plant life and animal life is already set by the universe. What we see every day is the seeds of nature and animals producing variations on a theme, and then finally facing extinction.

The trees and flowers go through their seasons of growth following the seasons of the sun. The animal part of all life follows the birth and death

cycle fixed by the aging process in nature, time. The destruction and creation process along the path of evolution.

The Ancients further believed that the divine spirit (spirit-soul) is not of nature. The divine spirit is the spark in human life that becomes conscious in the soul. It grows into a vita germ. Through this process, if the human allows it to govern the animal part, he will be the master of his own fate. The soul is not subject to the stars;the soul is free and can alter its course.   According to the Ancients, the soul can receive this spark (vita germ) at least three times during the journey of a life. The first time is at the age of four (4) months, then again, at four (4) year of age, and in the forty-second year of life.

If the spark does not germinate, the soul will continue to reincarnate. If the soul never receives the sparks after many lifetimes, it can be lost forever.

The great dance in the sky gave birth to astrology, that is, the study of the stars and planets. The study of astrology is the earliest journey into scientific reasoning known to mankind. Mysticism, symbolism, and geometer was the foundation of astrological thinking.

Though people in the western part of the world treat astrology as pure mysticism, without factual foundation, the eastern part of the world has been a little more aggressive in their pursuit of this knowledge.

I am going to explain to you what I have learned about the subject, and how it has affected my soul.

<u>**Reason and Logic**</u>

The experiences I have had are varied. I have been a constant seeker of truth, so I preceded to learn as much as possible.

The solar system impacts life on earth in a measurable way. Astrology has added to our knowledge of the Ancients and how they used it. The Ancients taught that at the hour of a persons birth, his location on the earth was influenced by the planet closes to the earth. They taught that conception and gestation are both affected by the astral moment.

The Ancients believed that "a name was a magic word." Just as the hour affects the person, the name given them also affects the course of their life. The name of a person expresses personality and quality of spirit-soul. The understanding was that the soul is free to choose its own desire and aim and could control the impact of the stars.

When I was in India, the local astrologer said that the reason I could discover a person's sun sign through observation was because I was spiritual. Implying that spiritual forces have something to do with astrology. Today, I am more aware that what a person believes affects the thought process. Thinking is a product of our emotions, self image, and beliefs. Therefore, in this area, I tread lightly because I am not sure of where spiritual force comes from. I am not aware of how much the brain and reason begins to pervade this concept as well.

I know that after reading several books on astrology, and by following the directions, I could discover a persons sun sign. I have also found that if you want to see a certain character trait in someone, you can see that trait. If what we believe determines what we see, then astrological reasoning is simply a product of experience and thinking.

What should you know about astrology? How can you keep from confusing your soul with labels and names that cause you to create vibrations that are foreign to you? Should you avoid astrology ? Should you condemn it in concert with the churches? Read on and decide for yourself.

Astrology teaches us that a person's sun sign,that is, the constellation the sun was in at the time of birth, would determine the personality traits of the person. The constellation the moon was in will determine the person's emotional state. The planet that was on the horizon, the rising sign, would determine the person's inner nature and personal appearance.

They also taught that Mercury was the ruler of the mind, Venus the ruler of passions, and Mars the ruler of speech and movement. Saturn as the ruler of discipline and time, while Jupiter was the ruler of childhood.

Some astrologers refer to themselves as sideralist because instead of finding the location of the sun, they are focused on the stars in the constellation. The reasoning is that the stars change every ten (10) days and are much more stable than a planet. They feel that their charts and predictions are far more accurate.

I am not bothered with the arguments between the two schools of thought; I am more focused on how either argument affects the soul. If the soul screams to be free of all convention, to escape matter, then it must learn how to deflect this reasoning process.

<u>**Reason and Logic**</u>

The Ancients looked at astrology first from the affects of the Grand Cycle and then they saw it from the Annual Cycle perspective. The Grand Cycle of the constellations procession is the measure of the quality and nature of each Age on the earth. An Age represented 2100 years, and each Age was governed by one of the four elements of nature. The cycle moves clockwise around the zodiac. The last Age was the Piscean Age, ruled by water. The Age before the Piscean Age was the Age of Aires, symbolized by the Ram and was ruled by fire. Each Age is found by continuing around the Zodiac in 2100 year intervals.

The next Age is the Aquarian Age. It will be ruled by air. The element that rules each Age is directly relevant to what progressive developments occur in technology, knowledge, and wisdom. During the Piscean Age, we saw the development of shipping and the exploration of the earth by water. In the coming Age, we are beginning to see the development of communication systems, spiritual evolution, and computers, all based on the air element.

The Annual Cycle moves in a counter clockwise direction with January (Capricorn) being at the top and February (Aquarian) following to the left and with Pisces in March.

What does all of this have to do with the soul? If the system contained truth, rather than reason and logic, we could say that it permits the soul the awareness of the possibilities within the environment of human life. It would remove many surprises about the evolution of the human experience.

I hope that you are beginning to see that

astrology is complex and can be misleading. This was probably one of the reasons it was banned by the church. Both of you can remember the times when I was doing astrological charts and sharing them with you. I didn't realize it then, but I was just going through a stage of personal and spiritual growth.

The basics of astrology are that the planet that is close to the earth at your birth will be your sun sign. For example, a person born during the winter when Saturn is close to the earth will be a Capricorn.

The traits attributed to a Capricorn come from the mysticism, symbolism, and geometer given to the planet Saturn. Due to Saturn's cycle and appearance, the Ancients felt that it ruled time and discipline on earth. Its cycle coincides with the number element of the moon, twenty-nine (29) years vs twenty-nine (29) days. Its affects controls time and the discipline in the cycles of the entire universe. An old planet, surrounded by colorful rings and had twenty-three (23) known moons. It looked capricious in the sky and was drawn with the symbol of the goat with a fish tail.

Its nature was tough and persistent and it had the sexual habits of goats. The typical person born under this symbol was seen as capricious, an old soul, and as an extremely disciplined soul. They represented the father of the zodiac, and was depicted as father time.

The planet Mercury was seen as having two sides, and it moved fast in its cycle. It was given the symbol of the twins and communication was its quality. The person born under its influences was seen as a communicator and as having a double personality.

Reason and Logic

The location of the moon in a certain constellation meant that the emotional state of the person would take on the character of that constellation. The affects of all the planets in the person's chart had to be considered. You can see that it's not a precise science and it requires a lot of translation.

A great device for explaining and predicting behavior, but accuracy is a problem. The mysticism of the Planets are in the words that describe them, the symbolism is the nature of the animal or thing assigned to it, and the season is relevant to the character of the person.

The geometrical affect is the number assigned to the planet and the degree it sits in the constellation. I don't know enough about astrology to discount it's affects upon the soul. I have found that sometimes you can guess a person's sun sign or ascendant just by observing that they behave or look like someone whose sign you already know, by using logic and reason.

This is an extremely perplexing moment for me. The power of the mysticism and symbolism in astrology is awesome. I know there must be some strain of truth in everything, but how it fits into astrology is beyond me.

The soul still wants to be free. Animals are fixed by the stars but humans are not! Because of free will, I feel strongly that human beings can control their own desire and aim in life; however, there is also a strong argument that the animal part of humans can be fixed by the stars. Just as colors and sound affect human behavior, the planets must have some affect, but we are not sure how or what it is.

The Ancients made up descriptions based upon

the behavior and appearances of planets. The argument is that those same descriptions appear in humans at birth when the designated planet is near the earth.

I have seen demonstrations of people trying to guess a persons sun sign by asking them their favorite color. I have used the device myself. By a leap of faith, you can follow the argument that each planet, with its season, represents a particular color.

The winter colors of earth are browns and blues, while early and late spring bring out the greens, yellows and reds. The summer months continue with the reds, dark browns, and light blues. The fall brings the rusty colors, the plaids, the darker colors, and falls into winter again. With a little practice, you can begin to make some educated guess about a person's sun sign by knowing the colors of the season they were born in.

One excellent way to shed further light on the subject of astrology and its affects on the soul is to compare it with the Eastern approach to explaining the great dance in the sky. Looking at China and some of the other Oriental approaches to explaining the universe and its affects upon human life can further clarify the issues.

The Chinese also look at the sky from a different part of the world. This is an Ancient system, but I believe that astrology predates it. A complete cycle of the Chinese universe is sixty (60) years. It has five (5) cycles of twelve (12) years each. They have five elements: Wood, Fire, Earth, Metal, and Water. The system is a lunar system because it is interpreted by the cycles of the moon as opposed to the sun.

Each one of the elements is represented by a negative or positive charge. Each of the twelve years has one of the elements. One year will be a negative year, the following year will be a positive year. Each year also has an animal spirit that represents it. A person born during the year of the animal designated, depending on the exact hour, will have the nature of that animal as their personality trait.

Only some of the astrological signs are symbolized by animals, but the animals are different. The mysticism behind this system is started by a story attributed to Lord Buddha, the great soul of China. Lord Buddha summoned all the animals to come together before he departed from the earth. Only twelve animals came to say goodbye so he named a year after each in the order they arrived. First came the rat, then the ox, the tiger, and the rabbit. Then came the dragon, snake, horse, and the sheep. Lastly came the monkey, rooster, dog, and the boar. Again, depending on the year you were born, this little animal hides in your heart.

The animal signs are combined with the five main elements that are combined with the planets. Wood is ruled by Jupiter, fire by Mars, and earth by Saturn. Metal or gold ruled by Venus, and Mercury by water. The negative and positive poles of each element is called the Yin and the Yang.

On the Lunar Calendar, the day begins at 11 p.m. and the twenty-four hours are divided into twelve section of two hours each. Each section is ruled by one of the animal signs. The time of birth is the ascendant and shapes the personality. The twelve signs are divided into positive and negative sides.

The rat,tiger,dragon,rabbit,monkey, and dog

belong to the positive sign, while the ox, rabbit, snake, sheep, rooster, and boar belong to the negative sign. The boar, rat, and ox, are with the water element. The tiger, rabbit, and dragon are with the wood element. The snake, horse, and sheep are with the fire element. The monkey, rooster, and dog, are with the metal or gold element.

The elements also reflect the changes in the seasons, water for winter, wood in the spring, fire in the summer, and metal in the autumn. The symbolism comes directly from the purpose and functional aspects of the element. From metal we get water, from water we get wood, from wood we get fire, and from fire we get the earth. Of course, all metals come from the earth, so the cycle begins again. The interchange between the elements is based upon power and control in relationships.

Metal is controlled by fire and fire is controlled by water. Water is controlled by earth, and earth is controlled by wood. Wood is controlled by metal and, again, the cycle starts.

The character in each person is with the behavior and quality of each of the elements. The hour of birth controls personality, but the element is the character. For example, people born in the year controlled by metal will be seen as rigid and resolute in expression while those in the fire year will be active, dynamic, and with plenty of ambition.

I know this is lot of information, but it will be helpful for you to recognize and understand it whenever the soul is faced by the mysticism of it, or the symbolism.

The geometrical affect here is the measurable

relationship between all of the factors outlined. According to this approach, a person's oriental chart will have the elements of your birth, the element of your animal sign,and the element of your hour of birth. It will also have the element of your month of birth. It also includes the element of your country of birth, the animal signs that are compatible and those that are incompatible.

Superimposed upon the animals, the elements, and the negative or positive charge is the affects of the moon. The moon governs the lunar month and has four phases. Each phase is made up of an element and is reflected in each animal sign. The phase the moon was in when you were born depends on the date of your birth. The moon phases start at different times of the month. The lunar year start in the winter, the presence of the first new Moon, so dates vary each year that starts the Chinese New Year.

The first seven and one half days are the new moon. The second seven and one half days are the first quarter or second phase. The next seven and one half days are the third phase or full moon. The last seven and one half days are the last quarter of the moon or the fourth week.

The new moon stands for renewal, birth, sowing, and awakening. The first quarter is for potency, maturity, and full growth. The second quarter or full moon is organization, harvest, collection and storage. The last quarter represents completion, conclusion, and hibernation.

The element that represents the new moon is wood and reflects the animals associated with that element. The second phase is fire, the third is metal and the last one is water. The Chinese believed that the lunar influences are the strongest because our bodies consist of three quarters liquid and the moon has a strong magnetic pull on bodies of water such as the rising and ebbing ocean tides. Plants and animals are also subject to this tremendous force.

In summation of this system, it started with planets just like astrology. The earliest date we have to start with the Chinese Lunar Calendar is 1900 though the system is more than forty-six hundred years old. In 1900, the ruling planet was Venus and it was a Positive-Metal-Rat year. The following year was the Negative-Metal-Ox year. The cycle continued as follows:

1902- Mercury-Positive-Water-Tiger
1903- Mercury-Negative-Water-Rabbit
1904- Jupiter-Positive-Wood-Dragon
1905- Jupiter-Negative-Wood-Snake
1906- Mars-Positive-Fire-Horse
1907- Mars-Negative-Fire-Sheep
1908- Saturn-Positive-Earth-Monkey
1909- Saturn-Negative-Earth-Rooster
1910- Venus-Positive-Metal-Dog
1911- Venus-Negative-Metal-Boar
1912- Mercury-Positive-Water-Rat

The second cycle of twelve years would follow the same order as above except the cycle would start with water. The third twelve year cycle would start with wood, the fourth twelve year cycle would start with fire, and the fifth and last cycle would start with earth. The information we have is not enough to show when the sixty year cycle begins or when it will end.

Keep in mind that these two systems, astrology and moon charts, of explaining the affects of the solar system on human life have been around a long time.   Generation after generation have followed the dictates of each as passed down by the Ancients.

The similarities can be seen in the use of the planets as symbols for events happening on earth. The Chinese use of the moon calendar is still one of the most accurate systems used by agricultural in modern times. Astrology is still under attack by the church, and is used to varying degrees by every walk of life.

Another system of explanation in the area of mysticism, symbolism and geometer is the subject called Numerology. The use of numbers as a designation for mystical phenomena is nothing new to many groups in America, especially the Jewish Religion. As to when the system attributed to numerology first started is not clear. The simple premise underlying the basis for numbers comes from the belief that the whole universe counts. That is, everything ever created is governed by number.   Numbers were used to quantify the vibrations in words. Words and number were closely related.

The sages in ancient Africa use to say, "Understanding may be awakened by knowledge of symbols and analogies, by knowledge of numbers or by absolute surrender of "me" in total fusion with self."
Number determines form. All forms started with the number one (1). The universe is all one (1). It is number that determines the forms taken in life and the journey it takes. Also, a person's name can set the desire and aim of the soul. If this is true, then a person must understand the mysticism and symbolism of their name to free the soul of its impact.

<u>**Reason and Logic**</u>

Under numerology, all names are set to number and each number has a meaning independent of its use. You will notice that in our previous discussion about the divine word, we saw how each letter was symbolized by a number. The number has the same meaning as the letter associated with it.

The following is a simple table of how numerology is organized:

```
A  B  C  D  E  F  G  H  I
J  K  L  M  N  O  P  Q  R
S  T  U  V  W  X  Y  Z
1  2  3  4  5  6  7  8  9
```

The meaning of each number is as follows:

1 = individualization, ambitious, career, leadership.
2 = associations, groups, center of attention.
3 = creative, self-expression, attractive, sought after.
4 = organization, respect, pillar of society, hub.
5 = freedom, sensuous freedom, travel.
6 = adjustments, domestic life, ordeal, changes.
7 = wisdom, aloneness, internal, within.
8 = wealth, board of director, president, material freedom.
9 = universality, the brotherhood of man, of the world.

As previously discussed under the divine word application, each line of letters is associated with a particular force in nature. A through I are the active/passive forces, J thorough R are the reactive force, and S through Z is the creative forces.

So, it is number that gives meaning to the words. It is number that contained the real meaning of life. Where do the numbers come from? Where did they get the meaning for each number? To learn where the numbers come from is the path to understand the essence of how mankind developed an introspective about self. One had to understand the developmental stages of the human body and mind.

The vast majority of the knowledge gained by the Ancients about the evolution of the human is through observation. By watching and listening to the growth process of a human life, they observed similar patterns and urges that could be identified at each stage of development.   A child at the age of ten will have the same urges and behavior patterns of a child of the same age. These urges could be discovered and described in great detail.

The Ancients set about developing a chronicle of human urges and concerns at each age of growth. Each age grouping was divided by seven year periods. A child from one (1) to seven (7) will have certain urges that would change when the child was between seven and fourteen (14);the change cycles would continue for every seven years until the person reached the age of sixty-three(63), then the cycle would start again.

Each stage was given a number that symbolized the description of that stage. The stages were outlined and labelled as follows:

Age: 1 to 7 7 to 14 14 to 21

Cycle: (1)   (2)   (3)

Age: 21 to 28 28 to 35 35 to 42

Cycle: (4)   (5)   (6)

<u>**Reason and Logic**</u>

Age: 42 to 49 49 to 56 56 to 63

Cycle: (7)   (8)   (9)

The numbers, one (1) through nine (9), have the same meaning as outlined before. The simplest way to put it is that a child in the 1 cycle is self absorbed, self centered, and is ambition about self. When they are between seven and fourteen, they start to join the group, the association, wanting attention.   From fourteen to twenty-one, the creative impulse of being begins. The need for self expression becomes paramount. Anyone who has raised children will recognize the teenager syndrome at this point of development.

Twenty-one through twenty-eight will be urges for organization of ones life, looking for respect, and overly sensitive to the treatment from others. Twenty-eight to thirty-five is a period when the soul wants to be free. It will seek sensual and physical freedom in all directions, including travel.

After the dispersion of wild oats, the person will fall into the thirty-five to forty-two cycle, and will suddenly be faced with all types of adjustments caused by circumstances created in the previous cycle. There will be a move toward domestication and responsible behavior.

The end of the twenty-eight to thirty-five cycle can be quite devastating for males. Some males become so disoriented and confused, they commit acts of desperation that could lead to a loss of the present life journey.

Upon reaching the age of forty-two, the human starts the journey within. A period of meditation about self, the internal vibration experienced, and

<u>**Reason and Logic**</u>

the why questions concerning the internal dialogue.

After this journey is over, the person is ready for the eighth (8th) cycle starting at forty-nine. A time for the accumulation of wealth and more of a leadership role within their own life. The fifty-sixth year will find the human now opening to universal principles of life, universal brotherhood. Once beyond sixty-three, the cycles start again, until the death of the body containing the soul.

The validity of these various systems of explanation about the human condition on earth will remain a mystery. I have outlined for you some of the subtleties of each system. This will help your soul understand what is happening within the systems that are independent of the soul.
They are all products of the human brain and are born of illusions, delusions, and falsehoods about the ultimate truth of mankind's existence on the earth. The error factor in the brain is pervasive, and because of it, the brain becomes the greatest obstruction to learning the truth.

The senses, if not understood, will cause havoc. A soul without this knowledge will be suffocated into darkness.

Chapter 3

PASSION: THE TYRANNY OF THE SENSES

To be free, the spirit-soul must understand the basis for suffering in the world. You have to understand and avoid the unmanageable world of the passions. The emotions that destroy the body, leaving the spirit-soul in a temple of sand. The feelings of anger, hatred, fear and desire are the sources of all suffering.

The senses in the body contain no knowledge or truth, they only affirm what is experienced. They are there to let you know that something is happening. How you chose to define that something and react to it becomes the nature of your moment to moment reality.

It has been clearly established that there is an automatic notion of crossing of the senses before they impact the brain. The crossing senses form the bases for illusion and error in the brain. The eyes may show that an event is happening while the nose or ears are picking up a different vibration. When the two or three senses clash and cross, the brain will create a form or thought that may not be accurate.

Thought itself is an impulse in the brain that measures distance. It allows us to see what we don't see. When the brain is measuring distances, the brain is comparing the length between ratios; similar to a mathematical exercise. The ratios are not clearly defined. Experience and knowledge affects the length of the measurement and because each person has had dissimilar experiences, knowledge accumulation, the measurements vary drastically. We have no control over our senses. When they run amuck, causing disastrous living conditions, we suffer.

<u>Passion</u>

A well conditioned thought process is supposed to be a good defense against the tyranny of the senses. In some circles of strong religious and cult doctrine, attempts have been made to deflect the senses but with little success. These attempts supply the basis for hypocrisy in America.

The terror the senses have dumped upon my spirit-soul has been devastating. Without the shallow and sporadic attempts by my parents to condition our brains against such terror, it would have been more dismal. The pleasure sensation has given me the greatest difficulty. That one sense has raped the very essence of my being. A lot of people are caught in the sensual sensation. What is shared here with you will help you understand the father you have known. The rape of being by the senses is a monumental challenge in our society and is directly tied with the advancement of civilization itself, in a direction other than backwards.

As both of you know, I had three brothers and four sisters. We were a very poor family. My father worked from before sun up to sun set when he had a job. My mother didn't work except for a very short time in child care.

In my sixth year, our parents would leave home for short trips, leaving my older sisters in charge. These were the times when the real life games would start. The senses took over and each of us were left to our own devices. Sometimes the older sisters, and some of our cousins, would want to play Post Office or we played Mom and Dad.

The Post Office game was poorly understood but Spin the Bottle was fun. These experiences were setting the future for my thought process, or the lack of one, about sex. Most of these games were a prelude to sexual knowledge. These games were the unleashing of forces that would dominate the illusions created by the brain for a lifetime.

Unfortunately, sensual confusion starts at an early age. This confusion becomes the hacksaw that constantly cuts across all future intimate relationships. It causes a severely flawed sexual beginning,resulting in unrealistic expectations.

It takes years to learn that the brain is an instrument of memory and comparisons. It is the seat of illusion and error. The Ancients knew that cerebral illusion is the most frequent aberration, and that being unaware of that fact is more than dangerous, it becomes pure horror. Out of this horrible fall from grace comes the basis for anger, fear, desire, and the destruction of the spirit-soul and body. The spirit of life never gets a fair chance to perform its miracles.

Stimulating the hot button in the body, started as a game. While Post Office was the main game, I was too young to receive a letter. By age eleven, the Spin the Bottle game took on a new meaning. Though the memories of the time are vague, this period of sexual awakening is too precious not to share with both of you. Yes, I had some of the same feelings you had to cope with, and yes, I still have them today.

When the old bottle pointed at me, it was my turn to go into the bedroom with a girl. It was probably one of my cousins or a sister. The girl laid down on the bed with her dress up. She pulled me on top of her. An erection was out of the question, but lying on top of her and being rocked from side to side was wonderful. When my turn was over, she pulled up my pants and sent me on my way. What was that all about? The thighs were warm, the panting sounds were intriguing, and the feeling of sparse pubic hairs against my leg was exciting. These were only dry runs.

The older we became, the mornings in bed with my brothers got more interesting. We use to wake up in the morning and discover little tents sticking up in the bed, the first formal erections."What in the hell was that?" It was so hard, you could knock it around with your hand and it wouldn't go down. What a rush! These were secret times, the boner times. Then the endless trips to the bathroom to play with the new friend begin. What a funny object! The thought of sticking it into anything had not occurred yet, nor had the pleasure of an ejaculation become a reality.
Here was this little protrusion growing on my body, never the slightest warning, it just proceeded to stick out.

When the boys got together, this little object became one of the topics of conservation. What in the hell do you do with it? Besides using it when going to the restroom, it was of no use. It just sort of hung around. The older boys in the family were beginning to experiment with theirs. Sometimes, the younger boys were the target. This didn't happen too often, but if you didn't get wise to the "boys will be boys," syndrome, you could be in trouble. You had to get the hell out when the older boys became amorous. What a state of affairs!

When the senses in the sex area really took off is not clear, but the first ejaculation was an earth shaking reality, an awesome revelation. What a feeling! The whole body would shudder and shake, it was great! My parents never sat us down

<u>**Passion**</u>

and talked about sexual development and what to do with this wonderful feeling. They never talked about sex. Our family referred to sex as "doing it, being nasty, getting some kutchipatche," or simply, the "ummn." The other night, a late night television talk show host referred to it as "the nasty" or "the wild thing."

Around fourteen years old the senses were into heavy affirmation of what the "wild thing" was about. A real live experience was still remote. Surely, there were a few dry runs but the earth shaking experience had not happened yet. What was happening supported the theory that most American males are pretty stupid about sex. The woman seldom reached any greater level of knowledge beyond the male. The sex drive was like getting a new computer with no instructions about its operation, or like getting a new bicycle without any wheels.

It would not be long before my real sexual education began. My first real job as the "Iceman" was the beginning of a new era. Did someone say,"Early independence?" Down at the icehouse, a few regulars talked with me about the ultimate sex experience. One woman in particular, who was the "Terminator" of infant sex habits, decided to educate me. She was in her late forties, a heavy set woman with a loud guttural laugh. She was a free spirit who would stop by my job on occasion and engaged me in small talk. The perfume she used was noticeable, and she wore red lipstick. She was an African-American women;her name is still in my memory. It won't be repeated here.

One summer day, the owner's wife decided to take me fishing with her to the famous Lake Isabella. She loved to fish and she was also a

dedicated business woman. She was all business all the time. The woman who visited me was her close friend. We invited her to come along.
This was my first time to go fishing. I couldn't tell the difference between a catfish or a blue gill. It was exciting to learn how to fish. We left early one morning for the lake, just the three of us. The drive was on a long and winding road that ran next to steep cliffs. The lake was beautiful. The owners wife had packed a lunch for all of us.

One of my jobs at the store was cleaning out the fish display case and packing it with fresh ice. It felt wonderful standing in the middle of a large blue lake trying to catch fish for the display case. Green shoots of grass all around me, there stood I, knee deep in water, casting a fishing rod. A new experience that would be a good memory for a life time.

Finally, I caught my first fish. What excitement, what joy! I was one excited kid! Removing the small catfish from the hook, I stared at its little face gasping in the air. So this is fishing. The owner's wife came over and placed a small hook in the fish's mouth.It had a long cord attached to it. She placed the fish back into the water and stuck the end of the cord into the water. She placed another little worm on my hook and went back to her location in the lake, about five hundred yards from me.

While standing there waiting for my next bite, there was a rustling sound of grass from behind me. I looked behind me, there stood the woman friend about ten feet from me. She said,"I have to find somewhere to go to the bathroom." Before I could avert my eyes, she pulled up her dress and pulled down her panties with her rear end facing my direction. I didn't know what to think or feel. I couldn't stop looking. I was in a trance. Two very large, dark brown buttocks were directly in my face.   Then came the paper wiping routine, the spreading of the cheeks and grunts of satisfaction. When she finished, she smiled at me and walked away.

What stirred inside of me was nameless. It was like a rush of excitement, a rapid heart beat, and a sense of wonderment. There was no erection but the strange feeling was slow in subsiding. Later that evening, we returned to the icehouse. The same woman who displayed her sexual parts, came to me outside of the store. She said,"Did you like what you saw at the lake?" I said, "Yes, it was a beautiful lake." She said,"I'm not talking about the lake, I'm talking about what I showed to you." I said,"Oh yea, now I remember, yes, that was nice."

She invited me to her house the next day during my lunch period (I had a three hour lunch break). The heart pounding started again. She gave me her address and quickly left. This would be my own little secret. No one would hear about this offer. Clearly, the old saying,"Curiosity killed the cat," was proper here. One dead cat was about to materialize.

At noon, the next day, the curiosity seeker walked down the street about a mile to the place where she lived. She lived in a little motel called the Lakeview Inn. My knock on the door was soft. In the background was a female voice,"Just a minute." She opened the door and stood there in a large red robe with no shoes on. She motioned for me to come in. We sat on the bed. It was a small room, so there was little else in it; a small dresser with a mirror, a bathroom, and a small ice box.

<u>**Passion**</u>

She started to talk about my job. She said that watching me work was fun. She commented on my hard work, and my handsome looks. She pulled me closer to her and kissed me on the lips. She said,"How did you like that?" I said,"That was good." Then she pushed me back onto the bed. She had nothing on underneath her robe. She said," Have you ever been with a woman before?" I said,"Yes." She said,"That's great, then you know what do." I thought to myself," the dry runs should count for something." We started doing the "wild thing" without much fanfare. Like riding a whale through rough waters, I hung on for dear life. There was no shooting blanks that day. We were together for about two hours. That wonderful, earth shaking feeling was experienced at least four times.

Walking back to work, I felt dizzy and could barely open my eyes. The brightness of the sun was blinding. I was shaking a little bit. The breeze felt good as it cooled my body. Life would be different after that day. The man had made it with a real woman in a real way. She continued to come by the ice house, and we did "it" a couple of more times. One day, she asked me for some money. When I said,"I have to asked my mother." She said, "Don't do that!" She never talk to me about money again.

Now the flood gate had been opened, the senses tuned to a new frequency, that is, how frequent would real sex start to happen. The senses found a fertile ground for discovery. That was the beginning of a sensual journey that would eventually lead to physical and mental destruction. Each new sexual relationship would create new illusions. My virile body needed serious attention and there were plenty of young women who wanted to teach me more about sex. I was like a child in a toy store. There were no limits;it was always just a matter of who, when, and where.

My spirit and soul were divided and trapped. My body knew that it could deliver the goods and it felt wonderful. I felt not one iota of guilt. It appeared to be the right thing to do. My spirit and soul had started their descent into the pit of hell, the senses. Feeling duty bound to satisfy the desire of every woman who made her intentions known to me, my senses were a sucker for a tight shirt, shorts, and suggestive walks. I felt good about myself.

Time would teach me that the very essence of my manhood was at stake in these meetings. That my spiritual and intellectual growth were jeopardized in a significant way. My identity as a person was irretrievably tied up in my sexual performance. A fate suffered by the typical African -American male, a sex machine. A tragedy of immense proportion, the true beginning of suffering. The reality of this tragedy would not come until twenty years later.

The impulse of being (sexual desire) is not understood by most civilizations. This life force in every living creature has an independent existence that follows its own rules. The rules are difficult to discover because the senses and the brain of humans keeps getting in the way. The force that operates inside of us and all around us shows itself in many different ways. Most, if not all, parents have no idea of what a child goes through when faced with the impulse of being, the sex drive. The bodies automatic mechanism for survival of its species is elusive.

By the time one becomes a parent, our own early

childhood sexual horrors have been hidden somewhere deep in our psyche. We didn't know anything because our parents didn't know anything. The entire sex act is shrouded in mysticism, crass and archaic symbols.

Being a truth seeker at an early age is a plus factor in the area of sex. The senses are so chaotic that the soul is at a lost. The soul gets lost in a place that represents darkness, but the senses give it the appearance of light. The senses teach us through their affirmation function that there is happiness in darkness. A truth seeker can find happiness in the light because they never stop searching for the truth. The soul believes it is happy because it feels good. Every sensuous cavity in the body is stimulated to assimilate happiness for the soul. This artificial stimulus factor also serves to support the bodies need for procreation.

The bodies only interest on this planet earth is the transference of sperm to egg so it may live again. A driving force in the body that creates emotional chaos until it reaches temporary satisfaction. The soul never had a chance. When the force is misunderstood, undisciplined, the soul misses its chance for enlightenment. The spirit force cannot lift it from the sensuous realm of the body. The control of the impulse of being (sex drive) inside of me was wholly lacking. As mentioned earlier, while in high school, I was a Disc-Jockey. All of the girls loved me. This was a crisis for my soul disguised as happiness.

My senses lead me to believe that it was fun, good times and happiness. What a life for a seventeen year old. There were different girls from all walks of life. A rainbow of colors and cultures passed through my arms. Emotionally touching, it felt wonderful, but the end results were devastating. A young Mexican-American girl came into my life during this time. Though she was older and had a little girl, it felt like love. Not knowing it was only in lust, I made a sucker move. As mentioned earlier, my parents were very tolerant of this relationship. A young white girl was after me during the same time. She could not get enough of me, she consumed me.

The girls in high school were like a fan club. As a celebrity on campus, it made me popular with everyone. As the student director of the band and choir, a local radio personality, there was nothing denied me. Interracial love was the theme of my life, though it wasn't my goal. I was in lust with all the girls and my spirit-soul was drowning in darkness.

All of the popularity was one of the reasons for being elected Vice-President of the school. The first African-American ever elected to the position. We had a student body of about forty-five hundered (4,500) students, less than ten (10) per cent were minorities. Pretty significant, though it didn't faze me at the time.

After starting college, my journey into darkness continued. Driving a school bus and working in radio, kept me busy. The senses would not change in their affirmation of the beauty and sexual attraction of the women around me. Unfortunately, there was a physical and mental crash on the way. The body was reaching its limits, the brain confused.The senses continued to wreak havoc.

Carrying twelve units of college work, driving buses mornings and afternoons, and working in radio in the evenings was an insane lifestyle. The sexual escapades continued with the little Mexican-

Passion

American girl from Texas. She wanted to marry me. The pace was too much for an eighteen year old. My plans were to move to Los Angeles after college and continue working in the press. There was no definite goal. My girlfriend and her child were sent to live with my sister in Los Angeles until my move could be completed. During this transition, my heart was broken in a serious way for the first time.

My girlfriend was working in a cafe in Los Angeles. I commuted on weekends to see her and the child. One Saturday night, around 9 p.m., I arrived at her apartment. She wasn't home yet. Walking across the street, I stood near a large tree and waited. Around eleven p.m., a car pulled into a gas station across the street from her apartment. It was a couple. They sat for about five minutes, then they hugged and kissed. A girl got out of the car and ran across the street into the apartment complex where my girl friend lived.

I walked up to her apartment door and knocked. She came to the door wearing her waitress uniform. She wore no shoes and she opened the door with a surprised look on her face. My camera was left at her place on a previous trip. With a slight glance in her direction I said,"I have come to pick up my camera." I walked straight ahead with my eyes focused on my camera. She reached for my arm. I pulled away. She said,"How long have you been out there?" I said nothing.

Picking up my camera, I turned back toward the door. She stood in front of me and she kept asking,"How long were you out there?" I pushed around her and walked out the door. She tried to grab my arm but I pulled it away again. I walked down the sidewalk. She was running behind me screaming," There is nothing wrong! It was only a friend!" "He only gave me a ride home from work!" I kept on walking, never looking back.

Wounded for the very first time of my life, it felt like a ton of bricks had fallen on top of me. My breath had stopped. There was something going terribly wrong. There were no tears then, I just hobbled away like a wounded bear. Riding a transit-bus downtown to the Greyhound bus station, I bought a ticket to Long Beach. Why Long Beach? I had no idea. The love child was stung and disoriented. We arrived in Long Beach around six a.m. Out of the depot and on to the street, I headed for the pier.

The sun was starting to come up. Walking to the end of the pier, my eyes stared down into the water.   Watching the ocean's ebb and flow, suddenly,little drops of water were hitting the surface. They were tears. Oh! What pain, what sorrow, what suffering. It was horrible. Making my way back to the bus depot, I eat breakfast. The next bus ticket was for home, Bakersfield. My life had stopped. College was over. The jobs were over. I quit! It was off to the Marines.

Yes, believe it, the United States Marine Corp. There was a war in South Vietnam. Some of my high school classmates had already died there. Why the military? Was it a death wish? What happened to me? The body and the senses had no more answers. How do you heal a broken heart? A soul lost in darkness, no light, no spirit. The soul wanted to commit suicide. It was in a terrible predicament.

One of my fellow school bus drivers heard about my intentions to join the service. Randy Abott was his name. He said,"Aubrey, I heard that you wanted to join the service." I said,"Yes, I'm thinking about doing that." He said,"We have a local Marine Reserve Unit here in Bakersfield." "You can go away for six months of training and then return to college. We have weekend meetings once a month for six years." During that time, when you dropped out of college, you were reclassified as one (1)A and sent to Vietnam.

The Marine Reserves wanted me. My parents were told about my decision two days before my bus left for boot camp. Marine Boot Camp began in November, 1964. The Marines introduced my mind, body, and spirit to a different type of sensual journey. My senses were now finding out how to affirm fear, and hatred. My soul was thrust deeper into darkness, consumed in the flames of evil, learning how to kill. My body became the gateway to untold torment, not pleasure, but pain. Oh! What pain and suffering. The brain was being forced to make the body beat itself. Threats of punishment and abuse were the order of the day. Screaming and name calling became the new masters of my soul.

We had constant exercising until we dropped in complete exhaustion every day. We were humiliated, shamed, and badgered into submission. Controlled for fourteen weeks: Told when to go to bed, when to get up, when to eat, and when to go to the toilet. Also, when to get dressed, what type dress, and how it was to be worn.

Drill, drill, drill, every day on the grinder. Close order drill, manual of arms, parades, molding sixty-four stupid males into one ideal, one purpose, one action. My senses were no longer confused. They were locked in shock, shut down for the first time. They couldn't cause any more trouble. My body was out of control, my soul was frozen, my spirit had abandoned me. What little light was there had left. Most of the time, there was nothing but soreness. My body barely moved. Every bone was breaking and every muscle was in spasticity. I was one emotionally sick turkey living in a hurt locker.

Reaching the age of twenty near the end of boot camp, one lesson learned was that I was not afraid to fight. I had no fear when physically threatened. Confused, dumb founded, and misinformed, but I wasn't afraid. One day, my Drill Instructor was going to hit me. He enjoyed slapping the troops around. That day he raised his fist toward me, I raised my fist also. We had a long and intense stare down and he backed off. He didn't bother me after that incident. This man would not be another man's fool. He wasn't going down without a fight. I didn't receive Private First Class Honors out of boot camp. That didn't matter to me, getting out alive did.

In my Bakersfield Unit, my first job was the driver of a fifty ton self - propelled tank. It could fire a shell more than seventeen miles. My Company Commander found out about my work in radio and with newspaper publishing. He made me the Company Public Information Officer. We worked in support of the troops in Vietnam. It was my responsibility to prepare publicity on our different projects. Reaching the rank of Sergeant, the six year obligation was completed without much fanfare.

You are probably wondering if my passions were still out of control. After boot training, the activity in that area slacked off in a significant way. I had more discipline in my life. In college, my grades improved. I made the Dean's list. I was still school bus driving and working in radio.

In the fall of 1965, I met your mother. She used to come down and watch me on the radio. We had many discussions about my life and all the women who were in my fan club. She understood that it was my life at that moment. My public life and my private life were one. She accepted me for what my life was then. I did not embarrass her with the knowledge of relationships with other women. Notwithstanding what the future held, it was complete honesty under the circumstances.

Our relationship was wild and unpredictable. We were children of the sixties: full of idealism, full of love, full of lust. We wanted to do what was morally correct. Our passions together were intense and unrelenting. I loved her. We were always together, talking about everything under the sun, having fun.

The senses were still in control. They were still a sucker for a beautiful women and your mother was no exception. I was committed to her, yet my senses and the crossing of notions in the brain continued their devastating impact on my life.

After we got married in 1967, I was convinced that there was going to be one woman in my life. We moved away from all the other rif raf. She meant the world to me. My jobs were still the same, and college life continued. The subject of law school was discussed with her. It became my goal. The idea of law school was to become a reality.

The control of illusions created by my senses and the impulse of being was stable. In my

<u>**Passion**</u>

American studies class, one of my class projects was a survey on sexual attitudes in America.

What type of sexual situations turned on Americans? Why this subject for a term paper? I don't have the slightest idea. A research plan was developed that included interviewing students and giving them a written survey. There were visits to different topless bars and porn shops to interview subjects.

Sometimes, we do something without knowing what the real motivation is nor the goal. This was one of those moments. It was during this interviewing process when the impulse of being (sex drive) showed me that it was incorrigible.

One of the interviews, with a female dancer who said she was a lesbian, did not end as expected. The questions were about why she preferred women to men as a sexual partner. She was about six feet tall, had dark long hair, and Mexican-American.

She had large cheek bones, looking more like an American-Indian. The interview took place, at her request, in her apartment. Her lesbian lover was present at the beginning of the questioning. She had short black hair and looked like a tough little man. She was a chain smoker and sat with her eyes glued on me.

To say that the interviewer was a little naive would be an understatement. It was impossible to realize the nature of the threat posed for this woman by me being in that apartment and talking to her lover. Ignorance is bliss. Anyway, the consummate interviewer continued with his questions.

After about thirty minutes, the little one left the apartment. They said something in Spanish that sounded like an argument. She looked at me and walked out. The tall one came back and set right next to me. She was wearing a dark top and a pair of shorts. She also handed me a glass of wine. We continued to talk. The impulse of being took control without warning. The women was all over me. There went one of my myths about lesbian women,that is, they all hate men. It wasn't that great. I never had intentions to have sex with this woman.

The little lesbian returned about thirty minutes later. She had fire in her eyes. She wanted to attack me. The big one protected me. My exit out the door was prompt. A slow walk around the block was necessary before getting into my car. What had just happened? How could I have been so weak? What went wrong? The body and the senses had no answers. The spirit was quiet. My soul was frozen. Sex occurred outside my marriage. All of my good intentions were shot to hell.

The survey was completed and submitted as my term paper. The teacher gave me an "A" on the paper and for the class. The findings on the survey were interesting. It clearly showed that the most sexually charged meetings for men was watching two women in a sex act. It also showed that most sex education was by trial and error, as demonstrated by me during the study. After that incident with the lesbian, my sensual flood gates were opened. There was not a lot of illicit sex, but the times it did happen, there was less and less remorse. The love for your mother had not ended. I enjoyed having sex with her. I had to hide each illicit encounter. My spirit was committed to her, but my soul and my body had started toward hell.

It remained a problem for me to control the impulse of being to the end of our seventeen year marriage. Even after she left me because of her strong religious convictions, my love for her was strong. What she did to the both of you was partially because of me. What my life had been with her over the years was redemptive, it was a good life. Passion and the tyranny of my senses had me under control. Ill equipped and ill prepared to face the explosion of my senses and the heat in my loins, there was never a chance. My brain, my soul, and my spirit were defenseless.

College life provided plenty of opportunity for self destruction and spiritual depreciation. This was the sixties and we were the flower children. It had its beauty and realism, yet no one was prepared for the consequences of too much of a good thing.

Bound for law school, my major as an undergraduate was Political Science with a pre-legal option. In between classes, the campus radio station was my hangout. Even this little station was a heaven for illicit sex. One of the students, a young Japanese American girl listened to my radio show. She would call and request the same song, something by the Doors. She invited me over one morning after my show and left her front door open for me. It was hypnotic and wonderful. This was pure lust at its best. Drowning in my senses and the impulse of being, the inexorable force had me.

This force is inexorable because it's unexplainable and undefinable, but it's there, looking for the opportunity to explode. College in the sixties was a constant challenge to what Freud called the libido. My libido or the inexorable force was never trained nor tamed. This is one force mankind shares with the entire animal kingdom. Widespread sexual paranoia and dysfunctional libidos have resulted in untold horror stories and it's still happening today.

My belief is that each generation of humans has tested the limits of the inexorable forces with varying results. In the sixties, we tried for new limits, thinly characterized as sexual freedom. College was the stage for the drama.

While in college, one of my jobs was driving a bus on the campus of U.C.L.A. for about a year. How a bus driver could become the center of attention of young female students is beyond me. There was a wonderful lady there who was working on her Masters Degree. She would wait for my bus each morning and then sit behind me and talk. There was more than one bus on the route. She choose mine everyday. She was an Italian-American, a very beautiful women. We would talk from the parking lot to the main campus. There was also a white girl who rode this same bus. She lived near the campus. Both of the women were great friends. As usual, the inexorable forces would eventually take over and the sex dance would start again. Trying to get an education, work two jobs, and entertain the needs of my senses was insane. A sex machine? Yes! Enjoyed it? Yes!

After receiving my undergraduate degree, it was on to law school. It would be a three year program that was extremely intense. You were not permitted to work the first year. Unless you were wealthy, you had to live on student loans. In the first year, we attended classes in the morning and afternoon.

<u>**Passion**</u>

We studied every evening until midnight, and all day on Saturday and Sunday. Finally, my senses were tied into the unknown. The brain, lost in muddle, was no help. The body still ached. What little time that was left was used to unleash the penned-up sexual fires.

Law students were a breed apart when it came to developing and dissolving dangerous liaisons. Dangerous because they were all at once intense and adventuresome, but once the release had passed, the deed was done, a new game was begun. Males and females had the same predatory instincts. As you now know, my second year of law school brought the birth of you, Virginia, and the last year saw the arrival of Eric. Both of you came from the sexual frenzy of the decade. Neither of you were planned by me. It happened to many couples. Some of those couples divorced immediately after law school. Your story centers on the pill that was not taken and the reluctant father who would not abandoned you.

Why your mother decided to have children during the most frustrating period of my life was incomprehensible. It was purely predatory. I love you both, but the idea of you took a long time for me to understand. My life was too consumed in my passion for my goals. After five years of marriage,the challenge of completing a legal education and passing the California Bar, meant that it wasn't the time for children. Ill prepared to be a parent, focused only on short term goals, and pleasure seeking, a family commitment was out of the question. The answer to what happened lies with your mother.

There will be no apologies here about the right or the wrongness of my behavior. Judge me as you wish, but you must know the truth. As compared to middle class standards, my life was out of control. My heart and my senses were true to the overblown needs of my body. The sexual attraction of my body for women was not understood. This was the biggest puzzle of my life. In my mind, the man was the hunter. There was never a suggestion that the man was hunted. Totally unconscious of the lure that my physical built was for women, my behavior made me a sitting duck. Middle class standards of conduct were not my cup of tea.

Much later in my life, my oldest brother had a long discussion with me about this phenomena in the Weldon family. My brother told me that the long line of Weldon men have been strong sexual attractions for women. It was because of our body size and because of our facial features.

We are handsome men. Natural breeders from Africa. His comments were noted in light of my trip to Africa. The Mandingo tribe and the roots of our ancestors supported his observations. Africans captured and brought to America during slavery were chosen based upon the size needed for doing field work and for breeding. That sounds horrible, but it was true.

The work on the plantations in America was too difficult for the Indians, many of them refused to do the work anyway. The answer: the African. Here lies the real truth about the sex machine mentality, the breeder. My ancestors were the answer for slave labor. This force, unleashed in America, is now a horrible nightmare for white America. The ideas about this phenomena have fueled the engine of segregation, hatred, and racial violence in America, the ogre of all to come in the nineteenth and twentieth century.

<u>Passion</u>

The conditions surrounding my lifestyle as an African in America were never questioned. My parents never said anything. My brothers and sisters were oblivious as well. My cousins all played into the same cesspool of deception and ignorance.

After law school, there were still illusions about the role of sex, the conditioning of the senses, the unleashing of passion. My policy of sexual honesty persisted. If a woman makes you feel a certain way, you tell her. There were no games, just straight forward conversation and a sensitivity to her emotions. It was just too damn easy.

After returning to the Marine Corp as a Judge-Advocate, the sensual aspects of my life slowed down. My commitment as a family man improved. To avoid hurting your mother, my conduct conformed to the middle class standard for quite a while. After receiving the negative results from the California Bar Examination, my life headed back into the toilet. My frustration level sky rocketed along with my alcohol consumption. The impulse of being returned with a vengeance. The quantity was less but the African stud was at it again. When my tour ended in the military, there was still frustration and disappointment with not being a member of the California Bar. It was no use. Working fulltime, keeping up with the social requirements of work and feeding my family, It was just too much.

My thirty-fifth year on this earth, the year of crisis for all males according to the teachings of the Chinese, the roof fell in again. My job was the general manager of a large bus company in San Francisco. There were about two hundred employees, three labor unions and about ten million dollars in assets to manage. This job represented corporate burn-out at its highest level. After three years, the feeling of being stuck became strong. The California Bar was still elusive. There was no where to go. My mind was falling into a whirlpool of psychic dramas, falling down, down, deeper and deeper into the pits of despair. It wasn't about sex anymore. Your mother had already told me that my sex drive was too much for her. It made her tired all the time and it was too much of a narcotic. She went deeper into a spiritual trip, my mind went deeper into a black cave. It was news to me but the next part of my journey was going to be spiritual.

Just a few more comments about the inexorable forces of life before leaving this subject of the senses. Societies have adopted many different types of behavioral codes to control these forces, some with extreme results. Some have tried with dress codes for females and males. Religions have preached dogma to match the intensity of the their moral code. This was the approach even before the Ten Commandments. At the other end of the spectrum are societies that have allowed the force to flourish, ending in wide spread disillusionment, disease, alcohol and drugs. There were some tries at reaching a happy medium in between the two extremes. In America, we have both extremes and those who struggle for the medium. This distance between celibacy and promiscuity is very short, so relapses abound along the pendulum between the two.

Cultural and racial differences in America make it more difficult to find ones own soul in the mist of it all. The Chinese have one attitude, the Mexicans another, and the Whites have varying degrees of paranoia about the subject. The African-American, obviously, has moved toward sexual freedom, and unfortunately, promiscuity. You will find similar level of promiscuity among the races in America depending upon the economic and social level of the group within the race. There is no empirical evidence to support this ratio, you just have to look around and experience what's happening. Furthermore, the term race is being loosely used here. There is only the human race. The color game is extremely ludicrous and dangerous.

The early Africans gave sacred names to the inexorable forces in nature. "KI-IKU" was the name for the reactive force "to be," and the impulse of being, meaning to raise up. This was the first force in the solar system. The second force was "MER" the law of attraction, the awareness of duality and fertilization. This force makes known the presence of two forces that result in fertilization. The first force becomes the second force. The third force is "SEKHEM" which was the recognition of the fire force that sparked creation. The fire force is destructive and out of this destruction comes creation.

The fourth force "KHEPER," was the force that causes the becoming of things. We see this force as existence, the relative reality. The fifth force is "AB-IB." It was the force that described the actions of the soul, it's desire and thirst.
The sixth force is, "TEKH," the absorption-fire principle of the soul, the impact of the destructive role of passion. The seventh force is the manifestation of the result of the causal impulse. It represents the reaction to the impulse of being. It's the force that set all things into reality. It is what we call the manifested universe.

The seven planets, the seven notes of the musical scale, the seven colors of the rainbow, and the seven stages of human development are examples of the manifested universe. It also brought us the seven continents on the earth, seven days a week, and the seven seas. All of this is symbolized by the grand circle of all matter moving in a circle.

The seven forces manifest themselves in our lives every day. These forces react to other forces. They are the forces in the mating cycles, the sperm into the egg and the fiery destruction with the egg giving raise to creation - a new life.

The soul within us thirsts with desire for others and things. The fire of absorption, the senses affirming, and the level of passion rising and falling. These are the inexorable forces that you feel within your body and feel them erupt all around you every day. How can this be said in simpler terms for you?

Before there was a manifested universe, there was only the spiritual realms. There were only spiritual forces. There was only the home of the Great Spirit and it created all the other spirits.
One of the spirits created its own spirit without a relationship with the Great Spirit. The spirit created was not like the other spirits. It was disowned and rejected by its mother.

She was ashamed of what she had done and decided to cast the self-created spirit out into space. This self created spirit was all alone in space and because it could exercise the powers of its mother that came form the Great Spirit, it decided to create another spirit in its own image. Also it created a place for it to live, the universe.

There was a great reactive force in the heavens

("KI-IKU"), the splitting of the force into two forces that were attracted to each other ("MER"). One was positive in force and the other was negative The crossing of these two forces ("SEKHEM") caused the creation of the universe and planet we call earth. The life form created in matter and was placed upon this earth ("KHEPER") It became the spirit-soul in matter ("AB'IB") filled with desire and absorption-fire ("TEKH"). This body contained the same force that created it. It was the begining of the life and death principle on earth. It travels in circles just like all the other manifested matter, including the planets in the universe and the sun.

According to the ancient teachings, every since this life form was placed on this planet, there have been messengers sent by the Great Spirit that have tried to teach them about the true spiritual self, that the earth was not the home of the spirit.

This description of creation of the manifested world has been around for a long time. There have been many variations on this theme of creation. Whether it was the great Hebrew Moses or the teachings of the early African sages. The flavor and the quality of the story has had the same effect, the story of the solar system.

Further study will teach you there have been many tries at the creation of life on earth. Life has taken many forms on this planet before the physical manifestation of the spirit-soul. The earth use to be a grotesque place with grotesque life forms. The perfection of the inexorable forces to the level of satisfaction they are at now took a long, long, time.

The impulse of being is still unknowable, and the senses are still out of control. The brain can still be duped into vast illusion and error. Reason has not given the soul the answers it needs nor has our experience on this planet. The journey of the spirit-soul on earth is not an external journey. The truth about the meaning and purpose of life is an internal journey.

CHAPTER 4

HEART CONSCIOUSNESS...
THE PATH WITHIN

The period of my life between thirty-five and forty-two was a period of domestic adjustments and grave responsibilities. The relationship with your mother was now one of tolerance and pretense. Something had died between us; all that remained was the mourning and burial. What exactly died would not become clear to me for quite sometime. Sometimes the very force that brings a couple together becomes the basis of their final separation.

Our conversations about what our relationship was about was no mystery. She promised to open my mind to books, her first love. My promise was to teach her about people. People are about the senses, passion, rationality, and ignoble purpose. They are about disease, fears, hatreds, and love-lust. My knowledge about people was substantial and she knew a lot about books, books about art, travel, mystery, and politics. She also loved books about government, astronomy, and philosophy. We were both excellent students. Our journey together was adventuresome. After my irretrievable lapse into books and her mounting disgust with people, including me, the end was inevitable.

Sex cannot sustain a relationship, nor can books, there must be something more. Children are not relationship extenders as well. It has something to do with the heart of mankind itself. That is, this concept called the heart. When people refer to their heart they reach for their chest. The physical muscle in the body labelled the heart is responsible for pumping blood throughout the body. It works with the lungs, the air regulator in the body.

The mystic, symbolist, and the geometer's approach to understanding the phenomenon called the "heart" relates to some of the most controversial problems in mankind's understanding of self. The mystic concerns itself with the stories about true love, the heart's desire, passions affect on the heart,the tale, tale heart. The sun of the body, the central cause of all causes. The heart of mankind is the shared consciousness and unconsciousness of mankind. The heart of the matter in all that matters.

The symbols of the heart are abound, the shape of the heart on a Valentine card. The symbol of the heart in a book of medicine. The universal symbol for the heart is unmistakable. The geometer gave the heart the number seven, the holy number. Though it starts with the number eight, its total is seven. The reading of all the numbers would show that the heart is about a crossing causal phenomenon that contains movement and carries great possibilities, a part of the solar principle but lives on earth. The heart and life on the earth can be viewed as interchangeable. It's internal functioning of mankind on the earth.

The seven number makes the heart the manifestation of all the forces that brought the solar system into existence. It is where mankind relates or becomes "one" with the solar system. The heart is within us and the heart is all around us. It is the kingdom of heaven on the earth.

How do you find the heart on the earth? This is a very large question. I can only share with you my journey to find it. Your journey will be different, but the destination will be the same. The messenger who will come into your life to help you start on the journey within, will not be readily obvious. It will be a truth seeker and they will touch you ever so lightly. The journey will start near your forty-second year unless you had been quickened at an earlier age.

The messenger in my life was a lady in her early sixties. She was young in her spirit and was extremely sensitive to the feeling of others. We met at a private security company in San Francisco. It was a few years after recovering from the thirty-fifth year fall when we were introduced. She was a client of the security firm. In my capacity as an account manager, we worked together in late 1983. It was my responsibility to insure that the security for her buildings was properly staffed. We would meet for lunch about once a month. It was during these lunch periods that we had many stimulating conversations about cosmic understanding. Her mind and soul encompassed a large part of the universe. She was to be my teacher.

Her method of teaching was subtle but effective. She was a member of an organization called the" White Eagle Society," based in London. She also was a reader of the teachings of a woman named Betty Bethard of Marin County. One of the first books I read in the area of meditation was her book: "Being Your Own Guru." The beginning part was the most difficult. Being externally focused all of my life, my senses were locked into my environment, arriving at conclusions erroneously, creating illusions, and running in and out of other people's lives. A busy body in the true sense of the word. People were my joy. Singing, dancing and having long philosophical discussions were my greatest pleasures. My brain was locked into the nonsense of peoples thoughts and behavior. Now, there was a need to go within myself to find myself.

Meditation was the key! There were all kinds of approaches to meditation, but the instructions in Betty's book were helpful. She recommends that you should set aside a place in your home or apartment where you go to for meditation only. My selection was a place in the corner of my bedroom facing toward the east, the direction of the rising sun. The idea of facing east has a lot of merit. The strongest amount of energy in the morning comes from the east. Some religious prayer position are facing to the east. Some teachers even recommend that you face your bed to the east because it will help you to sleep deeper and to dream deeper.

How you sit when you meditate is important in some practices not so important in others. You may sit in a chair with feet on the floor or you may sit on a stool with your legs folded comfortably underneath. Regardless of how you sit, just insure that you are comfortable. There were many variations at the beginning. Finally, I made a special stool for me. Some meditation practices recommend that you use a candle to settle your focus, and to use incense to start the senses for prayer. Again, you will experiment with a lot of different procedures and artifacts until you find what's comfortable for you. The use of music is also encouraged in some practices. Complete silence is ideal. Use of the "OM" sound on tape was helpful.

It took about a year for me to find the right combination that permitted internal travel. It may take you longer. It just depends on how much external dependency you have to get rid of; this is not an easy process. After a year, my ideal routine was to get up around five-thirty in the morning, exercise for about twenty minutes. Shave, shower, and afterward, spend about twenty minutes in meditation. After finishing the morning ritual, the rest of the day was met with joy and peace within.

Before arriving at this stage of mediational living, there were many side trips and readings along the way. There was the studying of various religious practices in the world. The reading of books by Shirley MacLaine, Jane Roberts and Shakti Gawain. Also, I read Gandhi, Togore, and Levi. There were travels to some resorts where only health food is served and meditation is encouraged alone with a massage.

There is this wonderful place called Harbin Hot Springs in Northern California. There were hiking trails, cold pools, hot pools, and warm pools at Harbin. There were areas for meditation and for nude sunbathing. It was here that my first experience of feeling a spirit-soul without a body happened. It happened in the hot pool and cold pool. The hot water is fed by a natural spring and was extremely hot. The cold water is also fed by a natural spring. First it was into the hot pool and then into the cold pool. This was done about five or six times.

My body became completely neutralized. It locked in a suspended state. This allowed my spirit-soul to soar freely. It moved all around. Free to go up to the stars, to fly through the air, to sit among the trees. It was free. Then there were the long hours of meditation in the warm pool. The road to complete relaxation was bumpy at first.

<u>Heart Consciousness</u>

The most important facets of meditation is getting in touch with the "little voice" within. People talked about this little voice, but it was hard for a nonbeliever. There was never a quiet moment in my insides. When it did happen, the external kid was not ready. At first, there is shock. Then there is amazement about the relevation. Before that happened, there was a need to clear my spirit-soul of a lot of confusion, hatred, and fear.

To clear your spirit-soul you must forgive everyone who you felt had hurt you in the past, and that you must forgive yourself for any wrongful conduct you had done. This was tough to deal with because of the anger within me.

One had to figure out who those people were that hurt you. What type of hidden hatred or fear did you feel. Once you have determined who all the people are and what the bone of contention is, you will be ready to take the next step. You didn't have to talk to the people unless you wanted to. If the person was dead, that presented a more pressing problem. With deep meditation, you can actually forgive them all, including yourself.
The most amazing fact about the process is to realize that the spirit never dies. The power of thought in raising a spirit, even from the dead must not be underestimated.

All phenomenon that exist in the collective unconscious never dies. The body may pass away, but the spirit is forever. The person who my soul needed to forgive the most had died seven years ago. He was my father. My father was a big man. He had large, strong, rough hands. His voice would boom over everything. He was clearly a Mandingo. The many times he had beat me had left their mark. The times he taken my arms and clapped them under his arms, put my legs between his legs, and then raised the belt to beat my naked rear end were not forgotten. The grunting, the sweating, the smell of liquor, he beat me, he beat me. Why? Oh why did he beat me? He hurt me! The beatings were frequent because of my problems understanding the desires of a child. At times, I was just too full of energy to give a damn.

Your Dad wasn't a bad child, curious yes, but not bad. There was a temper, that was for sure, but it seldom exploded. Honesty was my policy most of the time, and for that it was hell to pay. He still had to be forgiven for all the beatings and that included forgiving myself. It happened one morning around five-thirty. Deep in meditation, the call went to my father to speak with him.
His face and presence was brought into reality. What he did to me was discussed. The pain, the hatred, and the fear were talked about. He was forgiven. It was all right. What happened was over. There were no reasons for hating him anymore, he must forgive me. He did. There was no crying for him at his death, but now the tears were flowing like a baby that very instance. Expressing my love for him and how much he was missed, gave me a feeling that we both, from that day forward, would live in peace. All the goals struggled for in my life, and the care given to my family was because of him.

After that early morning session, my life within changed drastically. There was a new sense of freedom. My life could go on. It was unbelievable.It was truly a beginning. The next few sessions in meditation begin to open new levels of awareness. There was no question asked that the little voice within could not answer. It was beyond belief. This moment was only shared with a couple of people.

Heart Consciousness

While in meditation, answers to the most complex problems in electromagnetic reality were given to me. There was some information about the wisdom of the Ancients and the role of the impulse of the heart in our daily life. After this miracle break through, I felt pure joy! The possibilities of life began to open to me like a bright sun shinning through a window. It felt like a wonderful secret inside of me. It made me happy. It made me laugh. It was joy, joy, joy.

Now, each day of meditation brought new strength into my internal life. You begin to see how easily the senses and the brain could create multiple thought forms that created their own reality. There was the realization of how the spirit-soul was separate from all matter. There was more awareness of the peace and joy within. The reality of the heart. There was so much to experience in this new environment. It was almost impossible to share it with others. What was found within me was not understood by most people. It was like the farmer who found a large diamond on his land. He sold the land but kept the diamond.

There was also the fisherman who drew in a lot of little fish in his net except one big fish. He quickly threw the little fish back in but he kept the big fish. It became more and more apparent everyday that what was found through meditation was extremely remote to externally oriented Americans. It was experienced by few but sought after by many.

The next step was how to live in the world and live in this new place also. This also would prove most difficult. There are so few humans who have discovered the heaven here on earth. The heaven within that is also dancing all around us. It was next to impossible to share the experience. There were only two people to share my discovery, my teacher and a wonderful companion, Marie.

Marie was also a teacher in my life about spiritualism. She came into my life after the destruction of our family. Your mother had moved out, leaving me as a single parent. Marie met me in the building where we worked. We had smiled at each other several times while riding on the elevator. Later, we were introduced by a student of mine in college who was also an employee where Marie worked. We got along quite well. She even sat through my class in Commercial Law. She wanted to learn and it felt great to help her. Her interest and mine were similar though there were seven years difference in our age. The seed is planted, a new relationship, will it grow in different directions? Who knows? Enjoy it while it lasts. In relationships between the opposite sex, tomorrow is promised to no one. It is only in the now moment that those relationships make any sense. Enjoy the moment!

Each new experience in spiritual growth was shared with her. Both of you were too young to discuss such matters. That was out of the question because your mother had a powerful influence over your minds, and any positive reality about me was forbidden. Marie helped me toward a greater understanding of heart consciousness. She showed me how to focus in that area every day. The senses and passion in my life are still strong but not controlling with a vengeance.

Prayer and meditation have become the balancing forces in my life. It was Mahatma Gandhi who said, "Prayer keeps the heart clear of passion." That principle is starting to work in my life.

<u>Heart Consciousness</u>

Heart-consciousness becomes a new level of awareness. Like the sages taught in ancient Africa, the reality of heart-consciousness has nothing to do with the reality of the senses. It is when you try to mixed the two that confusion and disappointment begin to affect your life.

So, how can one live in the realm of heart-consciousness, work in the realm of relative reality, and in the realm of the senses? You can't! Here lies the problem of attaining higher consciousness and having to live on the earth. To give you guidance here is difficult because my journey in the outer realms of relativity and passion has not ended. Prayer and meditiation are helping.
There is no easy answer here. Every day is a struggle for me. Now that Eric is out of high school and you are nearing your completion of the Air Force Academy, there is an opportunity to make choices consistent with my heart.

This is one area where your mother was strong. She made a commitment to her heart;she joined her church and tried to follow its teaching. Though it meant the demise of our relationship and the destruction of our family, she made a choice.
Almost seven years after the demise, that choice still leaves me sitting on the fence. My heart's in a good place now and reaching for greater levels of awareness. There is still a long, long, way to go. Why can't my life be committed to getting off the fence? Maybe during this discussion, there will be an answer for myself.

The challenges facing the spirit-soul are religious in their nature. The term religion means " to link back," to go back to your origin, the origins of the spirit-soul itself. In meditation, you will learn that there is something within that links back to all times. You must understand this truth, a truth that must be lived. It defies definition. It's what we are, it is our essence. The invisible and undefinable something that's within us and all around us. You must understand this thought better than any other explanation.

My religious experience in America has had mix results. To be born an African by appearance, in a society with European values and culture, and try to find religious meaning in it all, is a shock to the spirit-soul. If one was born in Africa and raised in the African cultural experience, one would link back as espoused in that culture. The same would be true if born as a European, you would link back in another way. This condition causes immense problems for those of us born in a country that links back in a way foreign to what our appearance says we are. This was the first hurdle to linking back. Through all the hurdles of linking back, regardless of the many different appearances, the origin we link back to is the same. You learn this fact in meditation and the sharing of these mediational experiences with others. You will find that no matter what the cultural or claimed race, the experience in meditation is the same. We are all one!

The oneness is that we all share the same heart, the same internal consciousness. Every Age of mankind, a Messenger comes to teach us about this one consciousness and what must be done to find it. Here is where the problems of being on the fence really gets challenging. To know the truth and to live the truth are two very different realities. It has something to do with the word "faith."

CHAPTER 5

THE KEY TO SALVATION IS FAITH

According to the numerological sciences, the word "Faith" is symbolized by the number eight (8), the same number for the word "God." The numerical value association with the word faith and the meaning behind each hieroglyphic teaches us that the "F" is about the breath of life itself. The number "6" is about becoming and ending, the circle phenomena in life. The letter "A" is about the great possibilities of life. The "I" is the me-principle and the "T" is about being on this earth. The "H" is about the causal factor in crossing phenomena. Literally, the word is about the breath of life at its greatness within each of us on earth and its passing on to another level.

This is really the academic approach to understanding the possibilities of humans on this earth. Thanks to the teachings of the Ancients, we can begin to get a glimpse of what great realities there are. The most educated of our society completely miss the point in this area.

We talked about the Messenger from the different Ages earlier. Jesus was the Messenger for the Piscean Age, the water element. Even the name given to Jesus was according to his mission on earth. Jesus means Savior. Jesus was given the number eleven (11). It is a Master number that identifies those who teach the gospel or who are teachers in general. The sum of the name "Savior" is three (3), and symbolizes creation itself. So Jesus was a teacher who came to teach the spirit-soul about its own creation and its own salvation. Appropriately enough, according to the numbers, salvation is the number five (5), the symbol for freedom.

Faith is the only way to free the spirit-soul from

its entrapment in matter. For those of us sitting on the fence, this is the greatest challenge, finding faith and living our lives within it. How do you find faith? Where does it come from? Here comes another one of those aging questions. People trying to answer this question have caused the greatest destruction to humanity. Since the Crusades, one group or another has condemned, burned, or tortured their fellowman or woman trying to show how real their faith was for whatever belief.

Nations of people are subjugated to slavery, placed on reservations, and murdered for the sake of some other man's faith. The symbol of the cross is used to kill millions of people. Is there no end in sight? I am afraid not, children. No one wants to be the bearer of bad tidings, but the future of mankind's salvation is as bleak today as it was during the Crusades. There are many reasons for this horrible condition. The reasons are irrelevant for those who have faith, those who can find the truth beyond reason. Jesus said, "The truth shall make you free."

He was a wonderful teacher and only through him will you learn the truth. This teaching about the power of the truth has been repeated thousands of times but few understand what it really means. The idea was taught by my mother, it was taught in my church, and I have read it in the Bible. What does it mean?

My understanding of this truth is that it's an internal truth. All about what we call our heart, the central spirit that runs through our spirit-soul. All about the Great Spirit and our connection with it, about the real problem of getting beyond forms and matter. How can one get beyond forms and matter? The guidance provided by Jesus is the same key that opened the door for every Age. As mentioned earlier, the Message is taught to every Age. The first and most important fact is you must understand that the world that you don't see is the only reality. The world that is invisible and undefinable, where all that exist in the material world begins. To call it the spiritual world would place a limitation or label on a place where no such limits exist. The mystic sees the spirit as the invisible force on earth that animates all life forms. The spirit has been symbolized by the symbolist as a ghost or energy. The energy that causes a reality to happen, what causes motion and rest.

The geometer would see the spirit as the number one (1). The spermatic-fertilization process that is parked inside you, and it is a part of the sun energy and travels on the earth. Being number one, it's the beginning point for everything in existence or not in existence.

Jesus said that the human should be "filled with spirit but lacking in human reason, for human reason is only reason and the soul is only the soul." The most important force in life on earth is your spirit, the energy that gives you motion and rest. It is the essence of the life journey. This further means that multiple thought forms created by the brain are without truth, they are only thoughts.

The spirit-soul on this earth must recognize that it is animated by the Great Spirit, but is killed by the body. The only real life is spiritual life. The spirit within the soul is light within darkness. Therefore, the desire and aim in life is to live so that the body and soul should become filled with the spirit. When filled with spirit, someday, there will be no need for a body at all. To be filled with the spirit becomes the true purpose of life. This is the lesson that is taught each Age. Some get it but most don't. The reason they don't get it is because of reason and the tyranny of the senses.

It is just too difficult for a person to forsake the love of the flesh and the fear of suffering. Most all who have tried have failed, except Jesus. When you look around and watch what's happening to other people who are without spiritual understanding, they have great reverence to the material world. You will find desire and anger. If you are lost in material gain, you will notice the absence of the spirit within yourself.

How can you find the spirit within your own soul? How can you make that spirit so strong that pure light shines from you and all around you?
A good starting point is to understand the word faith and then find it within yourself. The mystic would see faith as a strong belief in something that can only be felt, a strong feeling. The common symbols we see concerning faith used by the symbolist is the cross, the fish, and individual expressions of belief within religious orders. Of course, there are churches here, there and eveywhere.

The geometer would see faith as the number eight (8), the number for wealth, for the ruler, the quickening breath of life, the beginning and ending of all the great possibilities within us on this earth, the crossing into another realm. Jesus said, "He that believeth in me, though he is dead, yet shall he live and whosoever liveth and believeth in me shall never die." These words are the beginning of understanding what faith means. This assertion requires the believer to acknowledge that life never ends, yet all around you, there is death. All that is material will pass away. Everyone knows that the human body will not last forever. Jesus is talking about the spirit-soul. It shall never die.

When attending church at eleven years of age, it was hard to believe a word spoken or read. It was boring and empty. The music was good but when it came time to scare some religion into us, it was rebellion. It just didn't feel right. All the crying and moaning was too much to take. It was time to count each moment, look out the window, or read a book until it was over. The idea of never dying was a true abstract. All you had to do was walk up to the front of the church and get down on your knees. Four or five Saints, that's what they called themselves, would kneel and pray for the sinner. After about an hour of this moaning and crying, the person would jump up hollering and crying,"I am saved!, I am saved!" Some just stood there and cried. That was astonishing to me!

The Sunday for baptizing was even more ludicrous to me. Complete terror if you couldn't even swim. The thought of walking out into that river and letting someone duck my head under water was frightening. At age fourteen, my church experiences ended. It was time to go to work.

The nature of the spirit was not understood by me until the age of forty-two. A very slow process for me because as a truth seeker, there were questions about everything. It was difficult to trust anyone, including myself. How in the hell do you find your spiritual self? This was one lost turkey, my body had tried to kill my soul. This is where meditation made the difference. The beginning of spirituality, learning about the invisible something that exists, it was the beginning.

<u>Faith</u>

To understand how the body was killing the soul is the first step. The soul has a tendency toward suicide. The body is not there to save it, the desires of the flesh have nothing to do with the spirit-soul. The spirit can only save the soul if it separates from the body. That is, the soul has to divorce itself from the body. Now that's really heavy. How do you divorce the body from the soul?

Considering this new understanding of the senses and the brain, one can begin to see how the spirit- soul was always separate from the body. The problem was coming to that level of awareness. It was surely a leap of faith, an unquestioned belief. Faith is about unquestioned belief. It meant that all thought, all senses, and all awareness has to be in the same belief. That belief is that Jesus is the resurrection and the life. He came to the world, he taught us, he was afflicted, he saved us, and he won his crown, The Christ.

The Messenger of the Piscean Age came to earth to teach lessons that would result in his death. However, his death was only a symbolic act to prove to the people that life was everlasting. Of course, he came back to life after the third day. This entire drama was staged to prove that the Great Spirit's promise of everlasting life was true. If you believed what Jesus had come to teach, if you believed in his resurrection from the grave and the suffering in his life, then you will know the truth. You will be free. He proved the complete power of the spirit over matter;the spirit is the truth for all times. What is it? What does it feel like? These are legitimate questions and shall be answered. Jesus said, "Whoever knows everything but lacks within lacks everything." This statement directly attacks the notion that the brain's knowledge is superior to any other form of knowledge.

You can be a great airline pilot, a smart lawyer, or a skilled doctor. You could be a hard working construction person or a professional telephone employee, in the spiritual world it would mean nothing. Lacking within is a serious and tangible risk affecting every spirit-soul on this earth. What people lack is the knowledge of the spirit within and how it works, its power, its rule of life, and its complete manifestation.

Jesus taught that our true images that existed before we entered our bodies would be difficult for us to look upon. The image is the same one that has the same likeness as the Great Spirit.
It's not desirable to look at. He said that we could not bear to see it. It would be frightening and beyond all imagination. The Great Spirit's image is so bright in its light, our true image is hidden within it. It's the image that neither dies or becomes visible. Here is the reason churches find it so difficult to talk about something you can't see, can't hear, yet you know its there. How can you teach the message of this invisible spirit?

This becomes the purpose of life,to find the Great Spirit within and to recognize that you dwell within it. We all have to find this place within us and when you do, you will see that the world is without substance. The only thing of substance dwells within you. "Whoever finds self is worth more than the world." Finding self is the true mission of life. To find self, you must understand the nature of the spirit.

The question is what is the force inside of you

that permits you to walk, raise your arms, or shake your head? It is the force that gives you motion and rest. Jesus was asked,"What is the nature of his father?" He said,"He is motion and rest." That statement holds the key to understanding the force within you. The more you think about it, the more sense it will make. It is the only type of reasoning that will take you to the truth. When we sleep at night, or at anytime, we call it resting. When we get up in the morning and move about, that force is being used. The force is so all encompassing. It is difficult to separate it from us. We are a part of the force but it's separate from us. We call that force spirit. Its essence can not be captured by the mystic, the symbolist, or the geometer because it creates them.

According to the geometer, the word "force" is the number eleven (11), a master number. It's the number of the teacher. In this case, the teacher inside of you, the substance that makes you breath, allows you to start and stop, and to be creative. Simple to explain the force of life, yet it is so poorly understood. Taken for granted, we don't miss it until it becomes invisible again. The force in the visible world is only experienced by observation or how we feel. When we see material objects move or come to rest, we know that something had to move it and stop it besides gravity, a better known force. When we see a car move under its own power, we know that it is caused by a motor. We know that the motor requires a power source to work.

We also know that when we see another human get up and move or stop walking, there is a motor inside, and it to has a power source. Where the car need gas and spark plugs to run, the human needs the Great Spirit to function; the Great Spirit

<u>Faith</u>

is the source of power for all life on this earth. Undefinable and invisible, all around us, inside of us, all one force. The force we are trying to reach within us when we are meditating, the force that speaks with the little voice, all the same force. This all may sound crazy to you right now, but by the time you reach your late or early forties, it will all make sense. My body may be gone by then and you will want to say thanks for the warning Dad. It's all right, my spirit- soul understands.

As you tap into this power within, your life will start to change. You will feel yourself becoming more tolerant of others. You will start thinking in terms of "us" as opposed to "them" and "me." The oneness in all humans will be experienced. You will begin to learn the lessons of unconditional love and the role that it plays in your life.

CHAPTER 6

<u>LOVE BRINGS HOPE TO THE WORLD</u>

After many years of traveling around the world and visiting each of the six continents (with the exception of Antarctic),my understanding of the human condition has been enhanced. Working many different types of jobs, and spending time in many people's lives, the ultimate truth revealed itself to me.

The purpose of life is to understand the journey within, and find the correct path to perfection of the spirit-soul. Perfection in the sense that the many journeys taken by the soul, in each incarnation, is about learning the lessons necessary to purify the spirit-soul. The goal is to overcome the need to incarnate in matter. The spirits ascension to other realms of existence becomes essential. It seeks to be one with its creator.

The spirit is perfect through all times, but the soul is not. The soul has to contend with the body, the brain, and the senses. You now understand the reasons the spirit has ended up inside a body and the struggle that follows once it happens. All of the different institutions and systems created by mankind will not bring salvation. Faith is the only path to salvation and love is the only path to bring them both.

What is meant by the word "love?" You have probably noticed that it is used to describe all types of human behavior. Those applications were never acceptable to me and that includes the approaches taken by most churches.

Over the generations of mankind, the mystics have showered the world with all types of spirit evocation and have called it love. Some countries have evolved elaborate stories and theories as to why people meet and participate in bizarre behavior and blame it on love. Some cultures to this day will pick the bride and groom independent of anything to do with love, but most Western countries still use love as the main pretense for why people get together and create babies, or they just get together.

The concept of romantic love is relatively new to modern society, and is changing in form all the time. To understand what the word "love" tries to describe, one must go much deeper in thought. The stories the mystics told about love are varied and extensive. The symbols used to represent love are all well known. Looking at love from the geometers prospective could lead to some helpful evidence as to what it may be about. This will be where our next lesson will start.

Since the beginning of my feeble knowledge about love (having a personal and sexual relationship with someone you cared about), I have always felt that love and sex were one. You can clearly see the problems that this simple perception caused for my body and the spirit-soul. My understanding was wrong.

The geometer's number for love is nine (9). This number represents universal brotherhood. As you already know, the letter "L" means transformation, going from one level to another. The "O" is for the beginning and ending phenomenon in life, the breath of life. The "V" is for creation, it has both positive and negative forces that are necessary for creation. Of course, the "E" is for movement of force or just plain movement. The word love measures the transformation of the breath of life in a creative way. An energy force creating and moving from one place to another. It represents change in life, or the force of change. The word love symbolized the force that creates life and causes all the changes in life. The ultimate consideration and understanding is that life is love.

Jesus has said,"Love brings hope to the world." This means that without love there is no hope, no purpose for living. This is a crucial and critical factor about the evolution of humans. The Hindu have long held that love is life and that sex is simply an exuberant expression of love. Sex is a physical need of the body as a basis for its own reproduction, it has little to do with unconditional love. A selfish expression of the body for survival, love is confused with this need and the spirit-soul plunges into deep, deep darkness.

The major problem for modern society is that sex is seen as the driving force of life. On this earth, sex is the driving force and everything sex creates dies. It can't produce anything that lasts forever. The spiritual part of life is forever. This problem has bugged the hell out of the churches for centuries, and has caused untold suffering. This condition will continue until the end of time as we know it.

In one of the stories about the life of Jesus, there is a discussion about how Jesus received the title "Christ." It means to be anointed. The story was told that while Jesus visited ancient Africa (changed to Egypt by the Greeks) he went to the Temple Sakara, the temple of the brotherhood or the men who called themselves Sages. They lived in the first circle of society, heart consciousness. The story is in,"The Aquarian Gospel of Jesus the Christ by Levi." In one chapter of the book there

<u>Love</u>

is a discussion about the ordeals that Jesus went through while visiting the temple.

There were six ordeals given to those who wanted to reach perfection and be anointed as a Christ. Only one person has passed all the tests and that was Jesus. An ordeal is like a trial. The person is placed in different situations to see how they will react. If they acted in the correct manner, then they passed the ordeal. The early churches used to have a test for faith. In the early part of our legal history there are all kinds of ordeals for guilt or innocence.

There was one called trial by fire. If you placed your hand over a fire and after three days it didn't blister, you were considered innocent or thought to be without sin. Trial by water was similar to this one. In that ordeal, you had to place your hand in a pot of hot water, and as by fire, if it didn't blister in three days you were without sin.

The ordeal for Jesus was the Bar of Right. It was given in the Temple Sakara. He was tested for six (6) character traits. If you had all six, you could be anointed and given the title, "The Christ." The ordeals tested for sincerity, justice, faith, philanthropy, heroism, and divine love. The object of the ordeal was to see if the soul had reached perfection with the spirit. Jesus was the only person to pass all the tests. There has really only been one Christ on this earth and that is Jesus.

Divine love is the ordeal that is most relevant to our discussion. Divine love means unconditional love for everyone and yourself. It has nothing to do with sex. Divine love is what the word "love" means. Unconditional love in all aspects: the ability to love your neighbor as yourself, to love your enemies, to love your father and mother in heaven.

<u>Love</u>

How many people have you met that are practicing divine love? Probably none because it's so difficult. Celibacy is difficult to attain, especially at a young age, making the separation between sex and divine love more tenuous. This is not to say that celibacy and divine love are one, but a strong argument can be made that the lack celibacy prevents the spirit-souls departure from the body.

So, here we have the crux of the problem concerning love. Unconditional love is divine love, there are no strings attached. You simply love yourself and others because you are human. Jesus said, "Love one another as I have loved you." This was the essence of the request for humans to practice divine love. How can you love someone who hurts you? How can you love someone who abuses you? How can you love someone who hates you or attacks you and threatens your life? How can you still love them all? These questions have to be answered by each spirit-soul on the path to perfection.

What can be said to you, as your earthly father, to help you on this journey? I find it difficult to say anything because I have not passed any of the ordeals. As you have noticed, divine love has been the worst ordeal for me. Since reaching my forty-second birthday, spiritualism is just now starting to make sense. My sincerity is improving, my faith is stronger, and seeking justice with less treachery is beginning to be a reality. Conquering fear and learning to give more to others expecting nothing in return is still a challenge. Again, divine love has been the toughest hurdle for me to overcome. As a truth seeker, to know the truth and how to live it is still a challenge.

One of the better books on the various levels of

<u>Love</u>

consciousness is, "Handbook to Higher Consciousness." It has a wonderful discussion about where divine love consciousness becomes a reality in you life. There are seven (7) levels of consciousness inside of humans, divine love is one of them. The number seven was used extensively in the past to explain the various centers in the body. "Handbook to Higher Consciousness" extends the concepts to consciousness in a modern way. The idea of dividing the body into seven centers of activity has been around for Ages.

These centers in the body are Chakras, the seven centers of spiritual energy according to yoga philosophy. The Chakras are as follows:

First Chakra: spinal cord and nervous system.
Second Chakra: the region of the sexual organs.
Third Chakra: in the stomach area.
Fourth Chakra: in the heart and lung area.
Fifth Chakra: in the throat area.
Sixth Chakra: in the center of the forehead.
Seventh Chakra: on the top of the head.

These designations were consistent with the numbers for the manifested universe. Even the colors of the rainbow are related to each Chakra,

Red - First
Orange - Second
Yellow - Third
Green - Fourth
Blue - Fifth
Violet - Sixth
White - Seventh

The known planets were also designated by number or Chakra:

<u>Love</u>

Sun - First
Moon - Second
Venus - Third
Saturn - Fourth
Mars - Fifth
Jupiter - Sixth
Mercury - Seventh

In the Higher Conscienceness Book, the first level of conscience is security, the basic needs of the humans for survival. The second level is the sensual pleasures. The third level is the power center, the need for control over others and self. The fourth level is divine love, living unconditional love. The fifth center is the cornucopia or horn of plenty center. The feeling that you have all that you need to live. The sixth center is the awareness center, the place where you watch your mind and body in action but you are free from fear, you can't be touched. The seventh center concerns itself with cosmic existence, where you become pure awareness, or one with your creator.

You can see that it is closely tied to the physical functions of the Chakras. You must read this book! What is important here is to recognize that these various levels of consciousness are important to understanding the state of the world today. It goes back to the lessons of the Pyramid mentioned earlier. Then, you were taught about how the soul descended into matter; this was symbolized by the Pyramid.

Well, the first three levels of consciousness are the ones that live inside the Pyramid. In every society on the earth you will find that most of the people are suffering in the first three levels of consciousness. That is, they are addicted to behavior that traps them in one if not all three levels of awareness. When one can reach the fourth and fifth levels of consciousness, one can see the real tragedy played out in the first three levels. This tragedy will continue to be played until the end of time as we know it.

Considering this understanding of the Pyramidal Cesspool, it becomes extremely important for the spirit-soul to learn all the lessons necessary to escape these three levels. This is where the teachings concerning going beyond forms and matter become important.

All that we have discussed up to this point tie in at this juncture. The spirit-soul must transverse through these levels of awareness to reach perfection, to reach freedom. Now you can see why divine love plays such an important part of life, it is life. Divine love will get you out of the Pyramid. The opportunity to reach salvation through faith will become possible.

Learning to love yourself is the first step. To become aware of yourself through meditation,to give yourself approval, and to make a commitment to living divine love. The road to the heart is narrow and it is sharp like a razor. Few have made it, most will pass away trying. This is why Jesus said,"Only one in ten thousand will be saved!" As you both know, most people believe that Jesus came to teach peace on earth, not true! He said,"I have come to bring conflict on the earth: fire, sword, war. For five people will be in a house;it will be three against two and two against three, father against son and son against father and they will stand alone."

He said this because the spirit does not belong on this earth. His lessons were to teach the spirit-soul how to leave the earth. The only way the

<u>**Love**</u>

spirit-soul can learn that it does not belong here on the earth is to first discover who it is, and become one in spirit, with the Great Spirit.

A lot of what's being said here is difficult to digest now. It will all come to you in time. If not this lifetime, then maybe the next one.
You can see that the real meaning of love is only understood as divine love. All the other false representations of love only confuses and distorts the spirit-soul.

Finally, let's see how love brings hope to the world. Obviously, we need to know what "hope" means to understand this concept. It is easy to figure out. All we have to do is return to the ancient Africans.

The geometer gives hope the number eight (8). Is it starting to make sense? It even starts with the number eight, the crossing-causal phenomena. Then comes "O," the breath of life, beginning and ending. The "P" is the place where all matter parks. Of course, the "E" is about movement. It's got to be easier for you now to figure out what's happening. Number sets the stage of language and meaning. You must understand these lessons, they all fit together.

Hope means that all the crossing-causal phenomena in human life is a desire to further the purpose of life. All the energy directed at sustaining life is parked in this word. So, we see how desire on the part of humans to live within divine love creates hope. It creates a future.

The creative energy causes change within the spirit-soul, giving it a reason to go beyond the crossing of energy phenomena each day. All of this wonderful phenomena breaks down when people don't: "do unto others as you would have them do unto you, love one another as I have loved you,love your neighbor as yourself and love your enemies."

Behavior that follows those directions will bring hope to the world. You notice the word is behavior. It has nothing to do with just thinking and talking about it. You have to just do it!
The most important lesson here is to remember that sex is only sex. It continues the survival of the species on this earth but it does not bring you salvation. It does not bring you divine love. Pray for the day when you will no longer be a victim of the impulse of being.

Knowing all of this wonderful information is helpful, but how do you love in this world and have salvation at the same time? Jesus said,"Whosoever has come to know the world has discovered a carcass. And whoever has discovered a carcass is worth more than the world." Once you have found that the world has nothing to offer the spirit-soul, for it is dead, how should you live your life to reach spiritual perfection?

CHAPTER 7

AVOIDING SOUL SUICIDE ON THE PATH TO PERFECTION:DOING GOOD WORKS!!

Jesus said,"Be enthusiastic about the word, for the first aspect of the word is Faith, the second is Love, and the third is Good Works, and from these comes life." Clearly,the spirit-soul must achieve faith for salvation. It must live divine love for hope, and the rest of life is about doing good works.

All of the evidence would sustain the position that when the soul is without the spirit it becomes trapped in the body. The false impression of reality that has been portrayed by the senses is not enough to sustain the soul. The soul goes into a state that is similar to suicide until it can reincarnate. This is why the light of the Great Spirit must be found during life on earth.

The ordeals used in the Temple Sakara is to try to see if the soul was free from the darkness of the body by gauging whether the soul had the capacity to escape from the body, that is, was it filled with light?

One can live on this earth and be sincere about their desires for divine love. They can act with justice toward all people and not with treachery. Their belief in divine love should help them to do good works. The human can give to others unselfishly, and they should not have to fear anyone or thing. They can love everyone unconditionally. Most people on the earth live in the first three levels of consciousness: security, sensuousness, and power. The internal struggle to satisfy these desires are devastating to the spirit-soul.

Doing good works on this earth is one of the

paths to enlightenment. Jesus said, "In order to find yourself you must lose yourself." This statement is about the lessons you will learn when you find the "little voice within." You will learn that your spirit-soul is intertwined with all souls and that humanity is all one. When you begin to serve others, the light will come on in the inside. Doing good works needs to be defined in light of what the Word teaches about life on this earth. If faith and divine love is the essence of the teachings, then to do good works, ones focus would be on doing something that helps others with their journey toward perfection, helping them in reaching salvation and hope within.

Each spirit-soul is trying to deal with the growth messages received through experiences on its own terms. How can you help them without getting caught in the messages they are receiving? You might believe that the works you are doing are good while it could be extremely damaging to the other spirit-soul where you become apart of the message they are receiving. Some of the churches and cults groups are already making serious errors overlooking this fact. When you come into contact with another spirit-soul, usually by accident or by a planned meeting, all the external factors impacting the spirit-soul can cause miscommunications.

Most of the social programs in our country never do well because of the inevitable problem of perception and no spiritual understanding. Spiritual unemployment is still a major factor when dealing with people in the West. Their external orientation is suffocating the spirit-souls.

What good works can be done to help people to have faith? What good works can be done to help people toward unconditional love? One could join an organization that prides itself on helping others such as the Red Cross, Salvation Army, or Rotary International. There is also the Lions Clubs, the Masons, and of course, a religious group. All of these organizations pride themselves in doing good works.

After being a Rotarian for almost ten years, Rotary's fellowship of men and women serving others has helped me focus more on the importance of "service above self." Helping the poor, the sick, and the lame is a wonderful example of doing good works. Working in service to others is the key to living within faith and divine love. One important factor to remember is that" a good person's steps are guided by (God) love." This statement from the Bible applies to all people. Being of service to others will not make you a good person. It means that you must also follow the teachings of Jesus while serving others.

There are occupations in the Western world that are exploitive and have very little moral value for others. The old problem of "giving unto Caesar what is Caeser's"is still with us. While giving to Caesar, you must realize that the spirit-soul is being destroyed. The heavy emphasis on external orientation, on appearance and performance degrades the soul. By working in Rotary, a lot can be learned about giving unselfishly. The weakness in my own understanding of the nature of good works is being exposed. It has something to do with helping the sick and the poor, as Jesus said,"feed my sheep." It stands to reason that when you help someone else, expecting nothing in return, you are helping yourself. It's the recognition of the oneness in mankind, the presence of the Great Spirit.

To do good works you do not have to be a member of some organized religion or service club. The basis of doing good works comes from the teachings of Jesus and all the other teachers before him. As mentioned earlier, each Age has had a teacher, but for some reason, each generation of humans has to learn the painful lessons all over.

Well, there you have it. The internal journey you are both on will bring a lot of joy and it will bring a lot of suffering. Your commitment to finding out who you really are and your commitment to others will determine the direction of your life toward perfection. No group, whether it be a church, cult, or charity can show you the way to salvation. It is an individual journey and you must make it alone. Once you have found yourself, the Great Spirit will reveal itself to you. It will comfort you every day. Your commitment from that day forward is to do good works.

Peace, love and joy to both of you. It's been a wonderful journey.

Love,

DAD!

BIBLIOGRAPHY

ALDER, VERA STANLEY, The Finding Of The Third Eye

    Samuel Weiser,Inc.
    York Beach, Maine, 1970

BETHARDS, BETTY, Being Your Own Guru

    Inner Light Foundation
    Novato, California

BLAVATSKY, H.P., The Secret Doctrine (1 & 2)

    The Theosophical Publishing
    Company, Limited, London, 1977

BREASTED, JAMES HENRY, The History Of Egypt

    Bantam Books, New York, 1965

CAPRA, FRITJOF, The Tao Of Physics

    Bantam Books, New York, 1976

CAMPBELL, FLORENCE, Your Days Are Numbered

    DeVorse & Company, 1987
    P.O. Box 550
    Marina del Rey, California,
    90294

CAMPBELL, JOSEPH, The Hero With A
Thousand Faces

    Bollingen Series XVII
    Princeton Universiyt Press, 1973

CAPT, RAYMOND E.,The Great Pyramid
Decoded

    Artisan Sales, 1971

COOKE, IVAN, The Return of Arthur Conan
Doyle

    The White Eagle Publishing
    Trust, Hampshire, England,
     1985

CONZE, EDWARD, Buddhism: Its Essence
And Development

    Harper & Row. New York, 1951

DIOP, CHEIKI ANTA, The African Origin Of
Civilization

    Lawrence Hill & Company, 1974
    Westport

EDWARDS, I.E.S., Treasures of Tutankhamun

    Ballantine Books
    New York,1976

GAWAIN, SHAKTI, Living In The Light

    New World Library, 1986
    58 Paul Drive, San Rafael, CA
     94903

GOODMAN, LINDA, Sun Signs

Taplinger Publishing Co.,Inc.
New York, 1968

GOODMAN, LINDA, Love Signs

Taplinger Publishing Co., Inc.
New York (1970)

GORDON, IRVING L., Review Text In World History

Amsco School
Publications,Inc.
New York, 1965

GIBRAN, KAHLIL, The Prophet

Alfred .A. Knopf Publisher
New York, 1951

GLEADOW, RUPERT, The Origin Of The Zodiac

Castle Books . New York, 1969

GROF, STANISLAV, Beyond The Brain

State University of New York
Press, 1985

HOUTS, MARSHALL,J.D., Jesus' Two Sanhedrin Acquittals

Swallows Book Publishers,
1992, 31878 Del Obispo, Suite
608 San Jaun Capistrano, CA
92675

KEANE, JERRYL L.,PH.D, Practical Astrology

Parker Publishing Co., Inc.
West Nyyack, N.Y., 1967

KEYES, KEN JR., Handbook To Higher Consciousness

Love Line Books
700 Commercial Avenue
Coos Bay, OR 97420, 1975

KIERNAN, THOMAS, The Wisdom Of Gandhi

Philosophical Library, Inc
New York, 1967

LAU, THEODORA, The Handbook Of Chinese Horoscopes

Harper & Row Publishers
New York, 1979

LEVI, The Aquarian Gospel Of Jesus The Christ

DeVorss & Co.,Publishers
Marina Del Rey, CA 90294-
0330,1987

LUBICZ DE, SCHWALLER ISHA, Her-Bak (The Living Face Of Ancient Egypt)

Inner Traditions International Ltd. 1978

LUBICZ DE, SCHWALLER ISHA, Her-Bak (Egyptian Initiate)

Inner Traditions
International Ltd. 1978

MACLAINE, SHIRLEY, Dancing In The Light

Bantam Books, New York, 1988

MACLAINE, SHIRLEY, Don't Fall Off The Mountain

Bantam Books, New York, 1986

MACLAINE, SHIRLEY, It's All In The Playing

Bantam Books, New York, 1987

MACNEICE, LOUIS, Astrology

Doubleday & Company Inc
Garden City, New York, 1964

MEYER, MARVIN, W., The Secret Teachings Of Jesus (Four Gnostic Gospels)

Vintage Books, New York, 1984

MCDANIEL, STANLEY V., The Philosophy of Nietzsche

Monarch Press, New York, 1965

MISSILDINE, HUGH W.,M.D., Your Inner Child Of The Past

Simon and Schuster
New York,1963

ROBERTS, JANE, Seth Speaks

Bantam Books, New York, 1972

ROBERTS, JANE, The Nature Of The Psyche

> Bantam Books, New York, 1984

SUGRUE, THOMAS, The Story Of Edgar Cayce (There is a River)

> A.R.E. Press, Viriginia
> Beach, VA, 23451 1990

TAGORE, RABINDRANATH, The Religion Of Man
> Beacon Press, 1930

URANTIA FOUNDATION, The Urantia Book

> Urantia Foundation, Chicago,
> 1955

WALTHAM, CLAE, I Ching (The Chinese Book Of Changes)

> Ace Publishing Corporation,
> 1969

WATTS, ALAN, Meditation

> Celestial Arts
> Millbrae, California, 1974

WATTS, ALAN, Death

> Celestial Arts
> Millbrae, California, 1975

WATTS, ALAN, The Wisdom Of Insecurity

> Vintage Books, New York, 1951

YOGI, MA'H'ARISHI MAHESH, Bhagavad-Gita

Penguin Books, Baltimore,
Maryland, 1967

ZUKAV, GARY, The Dancing Wu Li Masters

Bantam Books, New York, 1979

ORDER FORM

Telephone Orders: 415-994-3230

Postal Orders:

Aubre' Publishing
213 Knowles Ave
Daly City, CA 94014

Name:____________________

Address:________________

City:__________ **State**______

Zip________

Price: $14.95

Sales Tax:

Please add 8.25% for books shipped to California Addresses.

Shipping:

Book Rate: $2.00 for the first book and 75 cents for each additional book(Surface shipping may take three to four weeks)

Air Mail: $3.50 per book

Payment:

__Check

__Money Order